Discover SLOVENIA

CANKARJEVA ZALOŽBA
LJUBLJANA

Texts by Karel Natek, Peter Skoberne, Miloš Mikeln, Majda Vukelič, Nina Prešern, Mitja Košir, Gojko Zupan, Sandi Sitar, Janez Bogataj, Darinka Kladnik, Branka Murn, Evgen Bergant and Roger Metcalfe

Text editing by Zdravko Duša

Photos: Agencija Vas 101 t.; Archiv CZ 20, 22 t.r., 54 m., 63 m.l., 82 b.r., 85 m.; B. Čerin 80 b.l., 81; J. Černač 101 m.l.; M. Feist 115; A. Fevžer 27, 32 b., 70, 89 b., 90 m.r., 100 m., 101 b., 102 t.r., 103 b., 107, 108 m., 109, 110, 111, 116; Fotolik Celje 82 t., 82 b.l.; V. Furlan 59 b.; M. Garbajs 7 b., 12 t.l., 22 b., 31, 33 b., 36 b., 37, 39 t., 46 t., 51 b., 52 t., 55, 56 t., 59 t., 65 m., 67 t., 71, 76 t., 85 t., 86, 87 t., 92, 102 b., 121; F. Golob 103 t.; Gospodarsko razstavišče 39 b.; F. Habe 9 b., 10 t.l.; S. Habič 19 b.l.; J. Hanc 61, 62 t., 91; ISKRA 40 r., 41; P. Janežič 11 t., 11 b.r., 13; C. Jeraša 22 t.l., 28, 72 t.r., 76 b., 80 t., 119 m.; J. Kališnik 54 b.r.; S. Klemenc 14, 15, 16, 21, 34, 38 t., 63 m.r., 93, 94, 95, 98, 112; M. Kranjec 18 m., 32 t., 35, 42, 47, 48 b., 67 t., 69 m., 99, 102 t.l., 118; M. Kurtanjek 87 b.; M. Lenarčič 13 b.; J. Mally 18 t.l., 90 m.l.; Mednarodni grafični center 54 b.r.; I. Modic 4, 10 b., 60, 101 m.r., 108 b., 117, 119 b., 120 b.l., 128; Narodna galerija 53, 54 t.; A. Peklaj 18 t.r., 66 m.l., 88; J. Petek 26; L. Pintar 10 t.r., 12 t.r.; R. Podobnik 8, 25 m.; E. Primožič 19 b.r., 23 b., 25 t., 45 t.l., 45 b., 51 t., 56 b., 64, 65 b., 66 m.r., 66 b.l., 68 b., 75, 77 t., 84; PRS 33 t.r.; K. Rapoša 117; REVOZ 38 b.; B. Salaj 50, 53; P. Skoberne 9 t., 114, 120 b.r.; F. Sluga 11 b.l., 30, 62 b., 66 t., 96, 120 t.; Slovenska knjiga 44; M. Smerke 45 t.r., 58; SNG Maribor 49; F. Stele 67 t.; T. Škarja 108 t.; A. Tomšič 12 b., 69 t.; UIRS 40 m.l.; V. Vivod 89 t.; F. Vogelnik 17, 79, 80 b.r.; Z. Vogrinčič 29, 33 t.l., 100 b., 113; E. Zavrl 83; S. Živulovič 66 b.r., 68 t., 72 t.l., 72 m., 74, 77 b., 78, 106. **Cover:** E. Primožič, I. Modic, J. Hanc, M. Kranjec.
Cartography: IGF Ljubljana

Editorial Board
Mirko Fabčič, Matjaž Kek, Jure Žerovec, Ksenija Dolinar, Cveto Jeraša, Kazimir Rapoša

Editor: Kazimir Rapoša

Layout and art editor: Cveto Jeraša

Translated by Martin Cregeen

Published in Ljubljana by Cankarjeva založba

For the publisher: Jože Korinšek

© **Cankarjeva založba 1992, 1993, 1994, 1995**

Printed by DELO – Tiskarna, Ljubljana 1995

CIP – Kataložni zapis o publikaciji
Narodna in univerzitetna knjižnica, Ljubljana

908(497.12)

DISCOVER Slovenia / [texts by Karel Natek ... [et al.] ; photos Agencija Vas ... [et al.] ; cartography IGF Ljubljana ; translated by Martin Cregeen]. – Ljubljana : Cankarjeva založba, 1995

Izv. stv. nasl.: Slovenija. – Avtorji navedeni na hrbtu nasl. str.

ISBN 86-361-0944-2

1. Natek, Karel
50049024

Contents

This is Slovenia

The expression "the Slovene miracle" first appeard in the international media **5** in the mid-eighties. At that time, when the collapse of the eastern system was still unimaginable, magazines throughout the world first wrote, with the feeling of having discovered a new world, and for the most part with undisguised sympathy, about a central European country between Austria, Italy and Hungary, which could not be included among classically understood communist states in terms of civilized standards, concepts of human rights, national income or economic programmes.

Then came everything that caused the eighties to end with hope and the nineties to start with concern. For Slovenia, this was one of the peaks of its history: four and a half centuries after Protestant clerics inscribed them among European nations with a translated edition of the Bible, the Slovenes gained their own State. After the aggression of the Yugoslav Army and victory in the ten day war, the slogan about a miracle was reinforced by a notion of the intelligence and exceptional organisation of the Slovenes.

In the end, of course, we are what we are. Slovenia is not only one of the youngest, she is also one of the smallest of the European countries. With two million inhabitants, she has only a third the population of Denmark and is half the size of Switzerland; but her position is all that could be desired. Along the foothills of the eastern end of the chain of Alps, at the very tip of the most northerly Mediterranean bay, open towards Hungary and the south, it is a natural hub of European routes from north to south and west to east.

This land has already been marked as a new State on the diplomatic map and on the maps of international organisations. Most foreigners − we are under no illusion about it − have yet to get to know us. Whether you come as a tourist, as a guest or as a business partner, ask, ask, ask.

Slovenia has lots of answers.

Cerknica lake in spring, Cerknica plain when the water flows out

The Land
on the Sunny Side
of the Alps

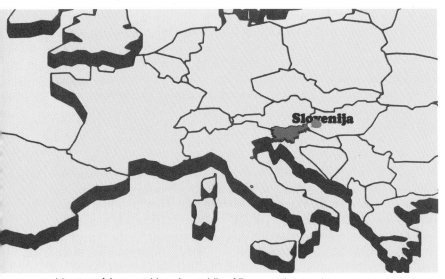

Meeting of three worlds in the middle of Europe: Alps, Mediterranean and Pannonia

Bled, Lipica, Portorož, Postojna. Next to Ljubljana, the best known names on the map of Slovenia, and often the only places on a traveller's tour of the Alpine lands of Europe and the western Mediterranean. There are places all over which you "must" see – Bled because of its lake, Lipica for its horses, Postojna for its famous underground caves. Tourist agencies will draw your attention to them, if nowhere else. What they usually forget to add is that here is the meeting point of three European worlds – the Mediterranean, Alpine and Pannonian. Slovenia, smaller than Sicily – the largest of the Mediterranean islands – has the geographic and cultural characteristic of all three. It is, in truth, a land for the connoisseur who appreciates a well maintained environment, who is accustomed to a civilised landscape created by generations of mainly farming folk.

Slovenia has eight more or less distinct regions

The Coastal Region

Slovenia has only slightly more than 40 kilometres of coastline, in the extreme north of the Mediterranean, in the Gulf of Trieste. Sečovlje saltpans were built on the delta at the mouth of the River Dragonja. Salt is now taken only from part of the pans, most of the area is now abandoned and provides a fascinating natural habitat for salt loving plants and a very diverse birdlife. The view to the northern shore is entirely different, where the spacious geometry of the salt flats is closed by the precipitous truncated face of Strunjan cliffs, the highest flysch cliffs on the Adriatic coastline. Here is the naked geological construction of the coastal region, a glimpse of the geological past, set off in good weather by a panorama stretching to the snowcapped Julian Alps.

The towns of Koper, Izola and Piran lie along the short indented coastline. They are typically Mediterranean at heart, a happy blend of Slovene and Italian. Koper is Slovenia's only port; the southern side of Piran bay, with Portorož, is made over to tourism.

Fiesa, the quietest bay on the Slovene coast

The Karst

Driving eastwards from the sea, through the hilly Slovene landscape filled with orchards and vineyards, one is suddenly faced with the next stage – a dark grey limestone wall. This is the edge of the Karst, a precipitous high cliff around 100 m high; a very pronounced climatic and geological boundary. The great contrast between the coastal flysch landscape and the sharp lines of the limestone will be best appreciated perhaps from the picturesque village of Osp. As one rises through Črni Kal to the plateau, the softness of the Mediterranean changes to a grey green landscape encased in stone – Karst. Many naturalists have studied this special landscape, created by the dissolving of limestone, and such interesting phenomena anywhere are known as karst phenomena, after it. A number of Slovene names have also been adopted into international usage, so the region between the edge of the Karst and Vipava valley is properly called classical or original Karst.

The Karst. A landscape which has given its name to a geological phenomenon throughout the world

The fragile beauty of "spaghetti" in Postojna caves

Almost half of Slovenia is limestone, so karst: more than 6000 caves have **9** so far been discovered on this small area, including three deeper than 1000 m. However, only a handful of the caves are accessible to tourists. The oldest "tourist" cave in Slovenia, and perhaps even in the world, is Vilenica by Divača. They were already collecting an entrance fee for viewing the cave in the first half of the 17th century. Among the most interesting caves on the classical Karst are those at Škocjan, inscribed since 1986 in the UNESCO list of the world cultural and natural heritage. An exceptionally interesting cave system has been created at the juncture of flysch and limestone. Two sunken valleys, through which the disappearing river Reka winds into Škocjan caves, can be followed into the largest underground canyon in the world, around 2.5 km long and 130 m high.

Another exceptional Karst region is connected with the Ljubljanica river, which flowed along the surface before the last ice age. Then, because of karstification, it dropped through a number of surface sections, which are still of course connected underground. It created a system of Karst polje and valleys with an intricate cave network, and seven major surface waters with

"Hanke's bridge" above the gorges of Škocjan caves

Proteus or the olm (*Proteus anguinus*) was discovered on the Karst – Carniolian primrose (*Primula carniolica*) grows only on the southern edge of the Alps

10 different names but, of course, all belonging to the same river, the Ljubljanica. Outstanding among the caves are watery Križna jama and Postojna cave, already famous for more than 700 years, and whose stalactite and stalagmite formations are viewed every year by around 800,000 people, earning them international fame.

Cerknica Lake is no less famous, an occasionally filled Karst polje in the system of the Ljubljanica river. There is a lake here for half the year in which one can fish and, in winter, skate on the frozen surface. It starts to disappear in spring and leaves behind a polje, where farmers cut hay through the summer. The causes of the drying out of this natural curiosity, already famous in classical times, were studied more than three hundred years ago by the natural and social historian, Janez Vajkard Valvasor. His report encouraged great interest; and he was elected a member of the Royal Society in London for his interpretations. Cerknica Lake established the concept of a Karst disappearing lake.

Rakov Škocjan, a 2.5 km long sunken valley between Cerkno and Planina polje, is a real Karst gem. What a delightful surprise for the traveller when, in

Massive natural bridge in Rakov Škocjan

Triglav, the mountain on the Slovene coat-of-arms. The precipitous north face

the midst of Dinarid fir-beech forest, the valley opens, dotted with picturesque karst phenomena: primordial sunken caves, natural bridges, swallow holes, springs, sinkholes.

Animals in the karst underground are adapted to a world without light. The most famous of them is the Olm (*Proteus anguinus*), endemic to the Dinarid karst and symbol of Slovene natural science.

The Alps

The arc of the Alps extends to Slovenia through the south east limestone Alps, so the ridges are sharp, there are extensive screes beneath the crumbling cliffs and, overall, there is powerful glacial formation. The image is completed by the characteristic white grey colour and the varied flora.

The western group, the Julian Alps, has an important close link with Triglav (2864 m), the highest peak and national symbol of Slovenia, also portrayed on the country's coat-of-arms. A wide area around it was declared a national park in 1981.

Three rivers cut into the Triglav massif: the Soča, the Sava Dolinka and the

Bled and Bohinj, pearls of the Julian Alps, have to a large extent retained their natural character

Savica Falls, source of the longest Slovene river – Zois bellflower (*Campanula zoysii*), endemic to the Slovene Alps – The magnificent Trenta valley below Triglav

White silence at Jezersko

Sava Bohinjka, and the picturesque glacial valleys of Planica with Tamar, **13**
Vrata, Kot and Krma open from the Julian Alps. The vistas to Jalovec from
Tamar, the mighty north Triglav face from Vrata, and the Martuljek group
from Srednji vrh, are among the finest views in the Alps.

On the western edge of the Julian Alps lies Bled, with its picturesque island
in the middle of the lake. The town and its surroundings have been an
international summer resort for centuries. The southern access to Triglav is by
the nearby glacial lake of Bohinj; while the western side is veiled in wild
seclusion. The village of Trenta is a delight, hewn from the centuries old
struggle for survival in the majestic but ungiving valley. Steep precipices fall in
a single sweep of a good thousand metres to the Soča, which is among the five
most unspoilt rivers in the entire Alps. The still untamed river, with a distinc-
tive milky blue colour, winds briskly through picturesque ravines, up to 70 m
deep on the tributaries and in places several metres wide. A number of
tributaries with waterfalls flow into the Soča, among which the highest, also
with the greatest flow of water of a Slovene waterfall, is the 106 m high Boka
falls by Bovec. Tolmin lies slightly to the south, the only town in this part of

Mountain farm in Robanov kot, on the way to the Savinja Alps

the Julian Alps. There are a number of major settlements by the eastern edge of the Julian Alps, including Jesenice, Radovljica and Škofja Loka.

There are similar picturesque panoramas in some of the smaller mountain groups of the Kamnik or Savinja Alps. The geologically young valley of the Kamniška Bistrica came in the wake of the last ice age, and three glacial valleys cut in from the upper part of the Savinja river basin: Matkov kot, the smallest and wildest; romantic Logarska dolina with its broad mountain scenery; and the more homely Robanov kot. Once the Savinja leaves the Alps' embrace, it calms down among the hopfields of the wide Savinja valley.

North of the central Alpine groups straggles the long ridge of the Karavanke, along which runs the state border between Slovenia and Austria. Southeast under the Alps lies Ljubljana basin, the most developed and heavily populated region of Slovenia. In addition to the capital city of Ljubljana, here are the strong economic centres of Kranj, Domžale and Kamnik.

Logarska dolina

Towards the east

Continuing eastwards from the Alps, the landscape changes ever more into undulating hills. The Alpine foothills are still cut with deep valleys, and Dolenjska is already attractively open. Here is the world of the Krka river, whose lazy current, tufa steps and abandoned mills set the seal to the entire landscape. There are only a few remnants left of the former extensive swamp era forest. The largest is Krakovo forest. The centre of this peaceful landscape is Novo mesto, above the green Krka river.

Towards the south, vineyards indent the extensive beech forests of the Gorjanci, a mountain ridge in which a number of myths and tales are still extant today. The southern slopes run through vineyards into Bela krajina, recognisable by its haybarns, and typical mainly birch stands created by the long tradition of gathering bedding for livestock. In between, one finds features, scattered like pearls, such as the cave of Kaščica, the source of the

Karst polje of Loški potok

Pools on the green Krka, natural bathing amid the Dolenjska hills

16 Krupa or that of the Lahinja river. The largest settlements in this region are Črnomelj and Metlika.

Bela krajina is bounded towards Croatia by the river Kolpa, which is here already a tranquil lowland river. Its upper stream, through a mighty canyon, is utterly different. There is a good deal still preserved here, the steep cliffs above the left bank being especially interesting. They are packed with fascinating rocky images, and the plantlife includes some real Illyrian specialities (e.g., false bellflower, *Edraianthus graminifolius*). The rocky cliff above the Kolpa continues into extensive fir-beech forest. Together with Kočevje and Snežnik forests, they are the largest forest complexes in Slovenia.

Central Slovenia is dominated by the Sava river, splitting it so to speak in two. It runs here through narrow valleys towards the mining and industrial towns of Zagorje, Trbovlje and Hrastnik. Towards the east, the valley widens and opens at Brežice onto the Pannonian plain.

Pohorje lies along the northern border, geologically the most Alpine of ridges, although rounded and forest covered in utter contrast to the bold sharp spectacle to which the limestone Alps accustom us. The best preserved

The Kolpa. River dividing Slovenia and Croatia

Pohorje, the green lungs of Štajerska

remnants of primary forest, as well as a beautiful waterfall, may be seen in the
forest of Šumik in Lobnica gorge. Maribor, the second largest Slovene city,
winds along the foothills. West of Pohorje lie Ravne, Slovenj Gradec and
Velenje; south, on the edge of the Savinja valley, Celje.

On the edge of the Pannonian plain

Kozjansko and Haloze are little visited regions of Slovenia, where the merciless
hardships of life have preserved true coexistence between man and nature.
Picturesque natural features are few here, life is too hard for such frippery.
Ptuj, the oldest Slovene city, nestles on Roman foundations beside the old
crossing over the Drava river. Every inch of the neighbouring Slovenske gorice
(small hills) is carefully cultivated, mainly of course vineyards on the sunny
hillside slopes. In between, one finds a number of smaller, but rather well
preserved mineral deposits, where the reddish surrounding soil advertises the
rich content of the mineral base.

Along the Mura river is the broad expanse of the Pannonian plain. Not so
much in the landscape, perhaps, which erupts in hills once more before

Dravsko polje

Storks in Prekmurje – Only one solitary floating mill remains on the Mura

Boundless Prekmurje plains

flattening to the plain, but especially in the unusual melancholy, mixed with a temperamental hospitality. These are feelings brought on by the lazy inertia of the Mura, endless fields, storks nests and, of course, meeting the local inhabitants. The further east we go, the more the melodious Prekmurian dialect mixes with Hungarian, which is spoken by the minority. Murska Sobota is the centre of the region.

We have only travelled some 200 kilometres as the crow flies from the Mediterranean and have experienced the most varied type of landscape, from the stone severity of the classical Karst and the limestone Alps to the flowing Pannonian plain.

Slovenes
through the Ages

Karantania

It will probably never be known for sure how much was preserved of the former inhabitants of the lands of modern Slovenia, of the Noricii, Illyricii, Venetii, the Celts and the Romans, when they were overwhelmed by the Slovenes during the migration of nations after 500 AD. In the 6th century AD, west Slavic tribes who had come through Moravia into the Eastern Alps, began to dominate the entire area along the Danube between Vienna and Linz and from the High Tauern below Salzburg to Trieste by the Adriatic. Around 200,000 people lived on this territory, three times bigger than contemporary Slovenia. In order to defend themselves from the Avars in the east and the Bavarians in the north west, they united around 620 AD into the Slav Principality of Karantania, centred on the Klagenfurt basin in today's Austrian Carinthia. In 745, they accepted the overlordship of the Frankish emperor and the Christian religion. From 869 to 874, they again lived independently, under their Slav Prince Kocelj, who had his seat further east, by Lake Balaton, and who even introduced Christian worship in the Slavic language and Slavic

Hallstatt situla, 6th century BC, witness to Celtic civilisation on these lands
Ljubljana was Emona under the Romans; remnants of the wall which ringed the city still bear witness to that time

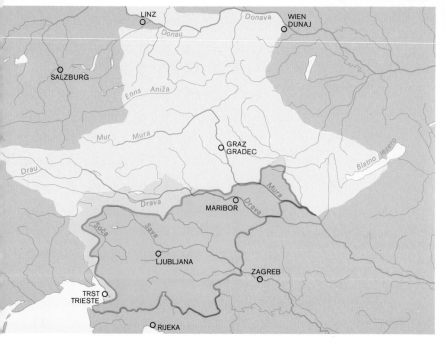

The Slovenes lived in the extreme southwest of Slavic lands. Since their arrival in the 6th century, their lands have been reduced by two thirds.
G. A. Kos: The enthronement of the Slovene princes on "Gosposvetsko polje".
Until the coming of the Franks, the Slovenes had their own administration and elected their own princes

script; before they were drowned in the empire of Charles the Great and his German successors for a millenium.

Birth of a nation

During this thousand years, the land was subjected to constant German pressure towards the south, to the warm Adriatic sea. By the 15th century, the northern Slovene national boundary had already had to retreat to a little above the Drava river. In fact, even in the 15th century, within the framework of the German empire, then already under the Habsburgs, they wanted to achieve greater independence within the Duchy of Celje, from the valley along the

Savinja in the centre of modern Slovenia, without in the end any success. The house of Habsburg held sway over the entire Slovene lands and Slovenes remained subject to the emperor in Vienna until the fall of the house of the two-headed eagle in 1918.

So the Slovene national consciousness was formed in conflict with the Germanic. Not militarily, there could be no sense in arguing thus with the giant to the north. The conflict was about language, education, about books, so it was conducted of course not by military leaders but by scholars, above all by ecclesiastics. Slovene protestant clerics published fifty books in Slovene between 1550 and 1600, the great majority of a religious nature but also a Slovene grammar. Two hundred years later, the first history of the Slovenes was published by the free-thinker, Anton Tomaž Linhart. In the following century, after the European "spring of nations" of 1848, when the Slovene intelligentsia published the first political programme, " United Slovenia", it expanded into à hard spiritual hinterland, in which the most powerful personality was France Prešeren, a poet on a par with the most spiritual of the European Romantics.

Before this, at the end of the Middle Ages, in common with the rest of Central Europe, Slovenia experienced great peasants' revolts, which several times laid seige to almost every Slovene town, and were put down only after really major battles. Together with Croatia, it protected the soft underbelly of Europe against the Turks, who had conquered Serbia and Bosnia, from where the tribes living there raided across the Croatian War March into Slovene lands as far as their northern border.

In the last quarter of the 19th century, the Slovenes also entered the era of modern politics. Three main political currents developed: the conservatives, who relied confidently on the loyalty of the Slovene nation to the Catholic church; the liberals, who were too often limited to opposing the interference of the church in politics, and the very weak socialists, modestly trying to catch the industrialisation of Slovene lands and the emergence of a working class.

At the turn of the twentieth century, Slovene politicians in the Vienna parliament initiated closer links with representatives of other Slavic states in

Celje. Ruins of the castle of the Counts of Celje, who even threw off the overlordship of the Habsburgs

Stojan Batič: Memorial by Ljubljana castle to the peasants' revolts. At the end of the 16th century, they were an important element in uniting the Slovene population against German feudalism

Map of Carniola from 1744, by Dizimus Florjančič. Carniolian lands in the Austro-Hungarian Empire were predominantly inhabited by Slovenes

the southeast of the monarchy, with Croatians and with Serbs from Croatian lands. They were united by the notion of an independent state entity of South Slavs within the monarchy: the Vienna two headed eagle should become three headed – Austro-Hungarian-South Slav.

However, Vienna, which was struggling with similar demands from Bohemia on the other side of the far flung Empire, showed no disposition to allow the Slovenes, split among four duchies: Styria, Carinthia, Carniola and Gorizia, to unite in a common state, and to give them, together with the Croats and the Serbs from Vojvodina, Bosnia and Croatia, the same independence as Hungarians enjoyed in Austro-Hungary. Even during the first world war, Slovene politicians demanded only autonomy, although Slovenes paid a high blood tax on the Soča front, one of the biggest of the war. When they were subsequently left empty handed, the mood of the Slovenes inclined toward an independent state of South Slavs which were then under the Vienna crown: it

Ossuary of St. Anthony in Kobarid, with the remains of the fallen in the first world war. The largest mountain battle of all time took place near Krn in 1917

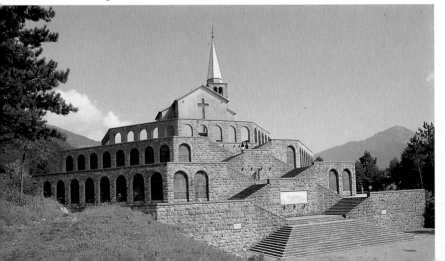

was to have consisted of the present Slovenia, Croatia and Bosnia and Herzegovina. In political documents and popular language, it began to be called Yugoslavia.

The First Yugoslavia

This state was declared on 27 October 1918 as a State of Slovenes, Croats and Serbs, with its capital in Zagreb and the Slovene, Anton Korošec, as president of the provisional parliament. The neighbours, though, cared little for Wilson's principles of national self-determination: Italy marched into Slovenia and conquered a third of it; from Croatia it took Istria and began to conquer Dalmatia and the Adriatic islands; while Croatia was squeezed on the other side by Hungary, and Slovene Styria by German remnants of Austria. The State of Slovenes, Croats and Serbs, as an illegitimate part of the defeated empire of Austro-Hungary, had no chance to survive. Its leaders took shelter under the Serbian crown.

At the beginning of the war in 1914, Serbia had declared that they were **23** fighting for the liberation of all South Slavs; but it understood this only as their annexation by Serbia. It thus established a very different state between the Danube and the Adriatic in the heart of the Balkans: unitarist and centralist.

The Slovene, Stane Derganc, a gymnast, was the model for the first stamp of the State of Serbs, Croats and Slovenes

The National Museum in Ljubljana preserves important evidence of Slovene history. A memorial to Janez Vajkard Valvasor stands in front

The major differences and contradictory interests amongst its nations could only be managed with a firm hand. Only in the autumn of 1939, when the shadow of the new war already hung over Europe, did Croatia obtain autonomy, while the Slovenes and Bosnians were dispatched with promises of something similar another time. Slovenia, of which one third suffered in addition to political pressure, also the nationalist violence of the Mussolini fascists and even greater ethnic pressure on a smaller part in Lower Carinthia in Austria, was catching up the stage of development of its Central European environment. It gained its own (although partial) University and other national institutions. Economic development was slightly faster in the last decade before the war but politically, a sharp contradiction arose among and within the different parties during these years.

In these circumstances, and in the spirit of a time governed by the marching column and large concepts of resurrection, the small illegal Communist party, banned since 1921, reformed by the end of the thirties into the fighting Bolshevik party, well organised and ready for the revolution.

24

The second world war

So Slovenia entered 1941, when the Kingdom of Yugoslavia speedily fell apart under the attack of Hitler's armies. Slovenia was occupied by Hitler's Germany which took the largest part, north of Ljubljana and the Sava, Fascist Italy which got Ljubljana and areas south of it, and their ally Hungary, which received the fertile plains along the Mura.

The Germans immediately expelled all the intelligentsia, the clergy and some ten thousand farmers, in whose homes they established Bessarabian and South Tyrolean German settlers. They banned the Slovene language in public, in schools and churches, destroyed Slovene books, and jailed and executed patriots.

In Italian Ljubljana and "Ljubljana province", the Italians initially allowed the Slovene capital cultural autonomy and at first tried to win the Slovenes to their side with kindness, with political and economic persuasion. So domestic politicians in this part of the country rejected the call to rise against the German and Italian occupiers that was made by the illegal communists in the

In 1941, Slovenia was partitioned among the Germans, Italians and Hungarians

Memorial to the fallen of the resistance movement 1941–45 (arch. Jože Plečnik)

Franja hospital in a gorge by Cerkno, which remained hidden from 1943 until the end of the war; allied airmen, together with partisans, were treated there

summer of 1941, after the German attack on the Soviet Union. The Communists, together with the Christian Socialists and other left-wing groups, organised the Liberation Front of the Slovene nation, formed partisan units and attacked the occupier. Established politicians, opposing the uprising and the left-wing Liberation Front, founded the anti-partisan home guard, called the white guard.

The partisans joined the all-Yugoslav partisan army of Josip Broz Tito, which was led by the Communist party. This party was eventually recognised by the British and Americans as an ally in the fight against Hitler and was supported, at first modestly but later with larger shipments of arms.

The anti-partisan white guard also sought recognition from the western superpowers but they were receiving arms from the Italians and later the

The resistance movement was victorious on the allied side through wide popular support (an historical record)

26 Germans. They were no different in this than other anti-bolshevik armies in eastern Europe, different nationalist legions, which took up arms after 1941, and especially 1943 and 1944, in their own struggle against communism.

The Slovene partisans fought a number of battles with the Germans and Italians which became legendary; monuments and isolated graves in the mountains and forests are a reminder of this. The Slovene white guard some success in the fight against the partisans, especially during 1944 and the beginning of 1945, but there was no escape from under the German high command. They stayed with the Germans until the last days of the war and they fled the country together with them, mainly to Austrian Carinthia. When the British returned around 10,000 unarmed white guard to their homeland in 1945, special divisions of the Yugoslav army executed them without trial.

In May 1945, the partisans marched over the former Slovene borders to South Carinthia and to the Slovene Littoral. They had soon to move from the area of Lower Carinthia below the Drava, which had been mainly Slovene in 1918 but was much more Germanized by 1945. They remained along the Adriatic and in its hinterland along the Soča. After a decade of argument with Italy, these formerly Slovene places eventually became part of Yugoslavia and Slovenia by international conference.

Tito's Yugoslavia

When, that same May 1945, "an iron curtain sprang up across the continent from Szczecin on the Baltic to Trieste on the Adriatic" as Winston Churchill said, Yugoslavia, and with it Slovenia, remained on the eastern side and "in one form or another to a large extent under the control of Moscow". All power was taken by the Communist party, it nationalised companies, industry, even the smallest, and large agricultural estates; it introduced a centrally planned economy and strict political control over all social life. Individual nations and their republics received extensive cultural and administrative independence but politically, power was centralised in Belgrade, as before in the Kingdom, mainly because the only party in power, the Communist party, was organised on strictly centralist lines.

After the quarrel between Tito and Stalin in 1948, which was more a rebellion against Moscow economic and political supervision than of an ideological nature, Yugoslavia drew closer to the West. Slowly it opened up its borders to foreign tourists, and to its own citizens. It began to introduce features of a market economy, and created its own socialist speciality, workers' self-management. It started to relax police control of society. Circumstances became ripe for more major political and economic reforms.

These reforms in the mid sixties, similar to what was beginning to appear in Czechoslovakia and elsewhere in Eastern Europe, brought substantial economic development, but, at the same time, the overall democratisation of society threatened the exclusive power of the Communist party. A counter attack was prepared amongst the leadership which, in 1971 and 1972, more or less forcibly removed the reformists. Many politicians and managers accused of "liberal" and "business" leanings had to go into early retirement or internal exile.

As a late echo of the reforms of the sixties, a new federal constitution was created at the start of the seventies and finally adopted in 1974. This new **27** constitution gave the republics more independence, but Yugoslavia's "leaden years" lasted from the counter-reformation in 1971 and 1972 until slightly after Tito's death in 1980.

To independence

A civil society speedily emerged in Slovenia in the second half of the eighties. Its creators in part took over existing institutions like the Writers' Association or the United Youth Organisation with its weekly, Mladina, and in part formed new ones, like the monthly magazine, Nova Revija. At the same time,

Brdo by Kranj, former residence of Yugoslav kings and President Tito, today a high category tourist facility and training centre

The start of the disintegration of Yugoslavia was characterised by intellectual ferment. The Slovene magazine, Mladina, opened discussion on all the burning questions in the former state

after backroom struggles in the governing Communist party and its affiliates like the Socialist Alliance, etc., reformists again took over. They prescribed radical treatment to the rigid party: to step down from power. The emerging opposition, which had started to organise politically in new "alliances" and "movements", at first refused to believe in this abdication, as did the orthodox Communist old guard, which watched with suspicion the activities of their young successors but made no anti-reform counter attack.

There were constant attempts to resurrect the strong hand of Belgrade, in economic as well as other, especially cultural, fields. The Slovene political establishment guietly evaded the economic pressures with political mano-euvring, although their own voluntary abdication was a painful decision. The cultural combat was public and loud. It was again carried on primarily by writers. Its effect was an acceleration in the political and national conscious-ness of the Slovenes and an ever higher level of dissatisfaction with a common Yugoslavia.

In the summer of 1988, the tension increased when three journalists of the weekly Mladina and a warrant officer who had handed over some relatively unimportant military information, were tried by military court. The process, conceived as a weapon to frighten the willfully deaf Slovenes, achieved the opposite: mass demonstrations, typically Slovene in being nonviolent but absolutely firm. Slogans about real democracy, political pluralism and free elections were joined by the demand for an independent Slovenia.

Over the next three years, to the end of 1991, one after another aim was fulfilled.

Sovereign Slovenia

The first step towards independence was taken in September 1989. The **29** Slovene Assembly then adopted an amendment to the republican constitution whereby Slovenia obtained the foundations of a sovereign state. At elections held in April 1990, DEMOS – a coalition of the most important new parties – obtained a parliamentary majority, and Milan Kučan was elected first President of the Republic by an overwhelming majority of the electorate.

A declaration on the sovereignty of the Republic of Slovenia was adopted after Belgrade threatened to impose a state of emergency. This act was supported by the people at a plebiscite held on 23 December 1990, when more than 88 percent of the electorate in Slovenia voted for independence. After the introduction of a series of measures, on 25 June 1991, with the adoption of the basic constitutional charter on sovereignty and independence, Slovenia also became de jure independent.

Because of the steadfast resistance of the Slovene leadership and the people as a whole, the final attempt of the Yugoslav army to obstruct the independence of Slovenia also failed. Hostilities ceased after ten days, and in October, the Yugoslav army finally withdrew from Slovenia, which had meanwhile taken control of its own borders and introduced its own currency – the tolar.

New Constitution

The Slovene Constitution was adopted on 23 December 1991, a year to the day after the plebiscite had been held. A legitimate basis for the new political arrangement was thus provided by the plebiscite, the basic constitutional charter and the new Constitution.

The new constitutional arrangement derives from the principle that Slovenia is a democratic republic and a legal and social state. Power is divided among the legislature, the executive and the judiciary. The highest body of legislative authority is the National Assembly, which has 90 delegates. A State Council, with 40 members, was also introduced as an advisory body. The President of the Republic represents Slovenia and is the commander-in-chief of its armed forces. The government, consisting of a president and ministers, is the highest executive body, and is independent within the bounds of its competences, and answerable to the National Assembly. Judges exercise judicial authority and their appointment is for life.

Elections 1992

After the adoption of the Constitution, which signified an essential break with the constitutional arrangement up to that time, since it guaranteed a democratic political system with a parliamentary form of state power, it soon became clear that new elections were approaching. Demos, the winner of the first democratic elections in 1990, had split into a number of new parties because of internal tensions. The Slovene assembly, which was still tri-cameral, found its work increasingly blocked, so that its legislative function was seriously threatened. Parliamentary elections were therefore held in December 1992, to the then 90 member National Assembly. The Liberal Democratic Party of Slovenia (LDS) obtained the most votes, followed by the Slovene Christian Democrats (SKD), the Joint List of Social Democrats (ZLSD), the Slovene National Party (SNS), the Slovene People's Party (SLS), the Democratic Party (DS), Greens of Slovenia (ZS) and the Social Democratic Party of Slovenia (SDSS). The president of LDS, Janez Drnovšek, obtained a mandate to form a new 15-member government, and he invited the SKD and ZLSD to join a coalition government. Until the middle of 1994, SDSS was also a coalition

The Assembly of the Republic of Slovenia adapted the new constitution on 23 December 1991

God's blessing on all nations,
Who long and work for that bright day,
When o'er earth's habitations
No war, no strife shall hold its sway:
Who long to see
That all men free
No more shall foes, but neighbours be.

Simbols of Slovenia: flag with coat-of-arms and anthem (F. Prešeren: The Toast)
The Slovene President, Milan Kučan, at the UN. Slovenia was accepted as a full
member on 22 May 1992, and almost exactly a year later, on 15 May 1993, into
the Council of Europe

partner, but they moved to the opposition when their president was replaced as defence minister.

Soon after the elections, several of the parties experienced various mergers and divisions that significantly changed the Slovene political space. Eight of twelve delegates left the Slovene National Party because of its loyalty to the government and most of them now form a new Slovene National Right party. Janez Drnovšek succeeded in bringing four parties together into a new Liberal Democrats of Slovenia party. LDS was thus joined by two parliamentary parties – the Democratic Party (although not in its entirety) and the Green-Ecological Social Party – and an extra-parliamentary party of socialists. The new LDS has 30 seats in the National Assembly. The Slovene political space has thus increasingly obtained an image delineated by three political options: centre-left, left and right.

Democratisation on the municipal level took place in December 1994. Elections were then held for the 147 new municipalities as the basic local communities which replaced the previous 62 municipalities. These had been essentially only an extension of the state, since they performed some 85 percent of their tasks on its behalf. Electors chose the members of the new municipal councils as the highest regulative body in municipalities, and 147 mayors. The results of the local elections provided a rather different picture on the local level than that on the state level, since right wing parties and independent candidates were most successful.

Minorities

The national tensions that led to war in former Yugoslavia raise the question of minorities in the Republic of Slovenia. There are no ethnic groups in Slovenia that have the right to self-determination and thus the possibility of forming their own state. There are two auchtonous national communities here, Italian and Hungarian, who make up approximately half a percent of the total population.

Prekmurje. Dobrovnik, a village with a strong Hungarian minority

32   According to the new Constitution, the Italian and Hungarian national communities are guaranteed the free use of their national symbols and, in order to preserve their national identity, they may form their own organisations and develop economic, cultural and scientific research activities, and activities in the field of media and publishing. They have the right under law to education and upbringing in their own language, and they are guaranteed the right to develop relations with the mother nation. The Italian and Hungarian national communities are also guaranteed representation in the National Assembly.

As far as members of other nations and nationalities in Slovenia are concerned, the law on citizenship enabled them to obtain Slovene citizenship until 25 December 1991 under very favourable conditions. The law on foreigners applies to those who did not make use of this. Among other things, this envisages permits for residence in the country and, in the case of employment, also work permits.

International Acceptance

Slightly less than a year after having declared independence, Slovenia was accepted as a permanent member of the UN (22.5.1992), and a year after that (13.5.1993) as a member of the Council of Europe. Today, in addition, it is a member of the Organisation for European Security and Cooperation (former CSCE), the World Bank, the World Trade Organisation, the Central European Initiative, the International Monetary Fund and NATO's Partnership for Peace. It has the status of observer in the parliamentary assembly of NATO and the West European Union, and has signed an agreement on cooperation with the European Community. The procedure has already begun for its acceptance as a full member of the European Community.

Economic Regeneration

Slovenia has slightly less than two million inhabitants, with approximately 851,000 in active employment, and an annual gross domestic product of around 12.6 billion USD, so around 6400 USD per inhabitant and close to 16 billion trade with the world. Two years after independence, economic trends in the state turned in a positive direction. Industry still has an important place in the economic structure of Slovenia, with interesting niches for almost all activities – with the major share of gross added value – close to 57 percent – being provided by services. The country has reliable and modern communications and PTT links, relatively good communal infrastructure, a long craft and industrial tradition and natural attributes which allow economic development in both manufacturing and service activities, especially in tourism.

Potential Workforce

A well qualified labour force, a high level of economic activity and a high percentage of women (46.6%) in the workforce, are important characteristics of Slovenia. Around 33,000 new professionals completed training schools and colleges in the first half of the nineties, around one quarter in technical

On the basis of the number of computers at work, Slovenia is part of the developed world

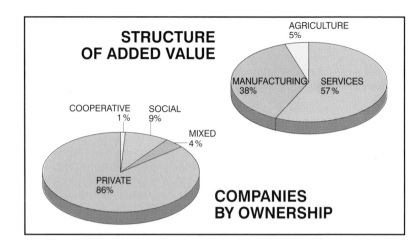

STRUCTURE OF ADDED VALUE

AGRICULTURE 5%
MANUFACTURING 38%
SERVICES 57%

COOPERATIVE 1%
SOCIAL 9%
MIXED 4%
PRIVATE 86%

COMPANIES BY OWNERSHIP

34 professions and as many again in management and economics. Ever more are also completing their education or further training abroad. Slovene business people speak English, German, Italian, French and Croatian.

Production work accounts for 47% of all employed in Slovenia, service activities 51%, and agriculture and forestry 2%. Recently, employment in private companies, as well as self-employment (private business) has greatly increased, especially in service activities. Unemployment, which rose considerably to 9% in the period 1991–1992 because of the economic crisis and the loss of markets, began to fall in 1994. Labour costs, without so-called added labour costs, average in the region of 8–10 DEM an hour at the end of the year 1994.

Traffic Crossroads

Balanced development policies in Slovenia have meant that – in addition to the two most important economic centres, Ljubljana and Maribor – a whole series of smaller business centres with appropriate communal infrastructure and hinterland have been strengthened. Nova Gorica, Koper, Celje, Murska

The road tunnel beneath the Karavanke overcomes the last natural obstacle to links with Central Europe. Motorways now come one after another (right)

Sobota, Jesenice, Kranj, Novo mesto and other towns have developed beside the main traffic arteries, along the main Slovene roads and railway lines.

There are two main directions: the first is the shortest overland link between France and Italy and the Pannonian plain, Milan–Ljubljana–Budapest. This direction is also the road and rail link with the Slovene port of Koper. The other direction is Munich–Ljubljana–Zagreb. The Karavanke tunnel, completed in June 1991, provides a new, excellent link between Slovenia and the system of European motorways. According to an ambitious plan, the Slovene traffic network will be entirely modernised by the year 2000.

With airports at Ljubljana and Maribor, and a rather smaller airport by the coast at Portorož, mainly intended for tourism, most important European business centres can be reached in one or two hours; and at most three to anywhere on the old continent. Ljubljana Brnik airport has connections daily or several times a week to Munich, Frankfurt, Zurich, Paris, London, Vienna, Rome, Split, Skopje, Moscow, Tiran, Istanbul and Copenhagen, by Adria,

Brnik — Ljubljana airport

36 Swissair, Lufthansa, Air France, DHL and others airlines. Both cargo and passenger traffic through Ljubljana airport is growing fast.

The Structure of the Slovene Economy

The Slovene economy covers almost the entire economic range, with representatives of almost all activities. Processing industries create 30% of the gross domestic product, followed in importance by trade, business services, traffic and financial services. Tourism is directly responsible for only 3% of the gross domestic product, although it is enormously important for the Slovene economic pulse.

There were 27,902 active businesses in Slovenia at the end of 1993, with a growing number of small private companies. Already, 94% of all companies are small, employing up to 50 persons. Large companies, employing more than 250, account for only 2% of all active businesses, though they provide nearly 58% of turnover, and 55% of all employment. New companies have recently been created, most dynamically in service activities, especially in the field of financial and business services and trade.

The Revoz (Renault) factory in Novo mesto, where they produce 80,000 vehicles a year (1992)

Four percent of the population are involved in agriculture, and the total harvest satisfies basic food needs

Business Infrastructure

The fact that Slovenia has its own shipping company, Splošno plovbo of Piran, an air transport company, Adria Airways, a stock exchange, the World Trade Center in Ljubljana and other institutions, contributes to the business infrastructure and real possibilities for business activity. The Chamber of Economy of Slovenia has an important role in establishing contacts among companies, and in providing other forms of assistance in business cooperation. Slovenia has also a good computer infrastructure, with the vast majority of companies and individuals in business having their own personal or other computers.

A number of foreign and domestic firme that assess the profitability of companies operate in Slovenia, as well as 3 foreign owned banks, and a total of 17 banks with permission to carry on all business at home and abroad. The largest are Nova ljubljanska banka and SKB banka.

Ljubljana contains the largest exhibition grounds in Slovenia, with a range of well-established international and domestic fair presentations. Kranj, Celje and Gornja Radgona also have major fairs. Slovenia is an ideal venue for various international symposia, seminars and professional meetings, for which

Ljubljana, with its Commercial Exhibition Centre, is one of the major fair centres in Central Europe

it has excellent facilities in Portorož, Bled, Radenci, Rogaška Slatina, Ljubljana, Maribor, Brdo pri Kranju and a number of other smaller tourist resorts, especially health spas. Ljubljana and Maribor are university centres, with departments also in other towns, and the best-known centres for training managers and foreign trade experts are at Brdo pri Kranju and Radenci.

Industrial Production

Production in Slovenia is diverse, with about 4400 industrial companies in all branches, with nearly 260,000 employees, making 1691 different groups of industrial product. Primary production – strongest and most successful in the iron working sector, manufacture of wood products, and the textile and leather industries – already existed here in the 14th century. Experience derives from the tradition of cobblers, tailors, blacksmiths, etc. The production of iron and glass on Slovene lands has even a tradition going back two thousand years.

Slovene design lines: Iskra telephone and Slovene textile products

Foreign Trade

Exports per head of population amounted to around 4200 USD in 1994, so considerably more than among competitors from southern, central and eastern Europe. The total export of goods and services in 1994 achieved approximately 8.3 billion USD, of which the export of goods amounted to some 6.75 billion USD and imports 7.20 billion USD. There is a positive current account balance. Finished and processed goods account for 90% of exports, and raw materials for one fifth of imports. The most important trading partners are Germany, Italy, France, Croatia, Austria, USA, Russia, Great Britain and Macedonia. The key export earners are industry, tourism and transport.

The most important groups of export products are vehicles, pharmaceuticals, furniture, textiles, whitewash, etc. We are, for example, among the largest manufacturers of trousers in Europe. Our automobile industry cooperates

Production of telephone exchanges in Iskra, which cooperates with the German company, Siemens

with the world famous manufacturers, Opel, BMW, Renault, Citroen and **39** Volkswagon. Slovenia has first class producers of skis and other sports equipment and footwear, and a range of other high quality leisure products, and Slovene producers have successfully fitted out Himalayan expeditions.

Slovene wines are celebrated, as are the excellent fruit juices, and Karst smoked ham, pasta products, vegetable preserves... Slovenia makes and successfully exports good steel products, particularly special steels, industrial non- metal products, such as the very high quality design crystalware – sold in their own retail outlet on Fifth Avenue in New York – as well as pharmaceuticals, equipment for the baking industry, airport fittings, high quality whiteware, tools, telephones, environmentally friendly insulation materials, etc.

Investment

Major facilities completed recently in Slovenia include the Karavanke tunnel, a number of power facilities and improvements to certain road links. Investment has also greatly improved PTT traffic, including with the introduction of mobile telephone systems. There have been major investments in industry,

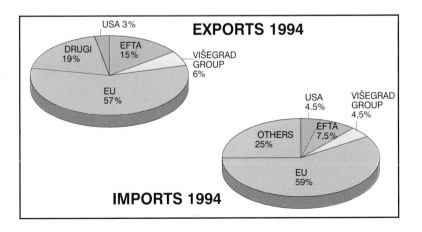

The port of Koper, the shortest route from Central Europe to the Mediterranean

40 especially in vehicle manufacturing, pharmaceuticals and the electro-industry, as well as ecologically directed investment. Most investment in tourism in recent years has gone into health tourism facilities, with major investment also in casinos. Private investment into small and medium sized companies has become increasingly important, especially in service activities, and in trade. There have also been a number of important investments in the fields of education, health and the arts – including an extension to the National Gallery, and the construction of a new Central Technical Library is also in preparation. The ratio of investment to gross domestic product increased last year to 19%.

Slovenia anticipates even more lively investment activity in the coming years. The economy is successfully adapting to new market demands. The Slovene economy is looking for foreign coinvestment especially in the fields of tourism, traffic links, electronics, furniture, the production of drinks and the chemical and metal working industries, in the production of steel, as well as other industrial fields. So far, the major joint venture partners have been from Germany, Italy and Austria.

The Ljubljana stock exchange is an innovation for Slovene business peopele

Economic Policy and the Tax System

Slovenia introduced its own currency – the Slovene tolar (SIT) in October 1991, which has become well established, is internally convertible, and has achieved a relatively high level of stability. In 1994, the average exchange rate was 79.4 SIT to the DEM and 129 SIT to the American dollar. The state has created a solid foreign exchange reserve in the last few years.

The tax system has been to a large extent brought into line with those in other European countries. Profit is taxed at a level of 25%, and income tax rates are from 17% to 50%. Employers deduct 26.6% of the gross pay of employees for social security contributions (pension-disability and health insurance and unemployment insurance), and employees 22.1%. So the ratio between the net take home pay of an employee and the total labour costs for an employer including all tax liabilities for an average monthly salary of 820 DEM in Slovenia is 1:1.93 (November 1994).

The currency with the international symbol SIT – the Slovene tolar

At the end of 1994, the process of privatisation (or the ownership transformation of former social companies) was formerly concluded.

Slovenia has a modern law on businesses, of the continental European type, and liberal foreign trade regulations. It is speedily adapting to modern solutions and standards which apply in the European Union, in which we wish in due course to be included, and the requirements of the WTO, of which we are already a member. In the next few years, a continued undisturbed process of relaxation and liberalisation to encourage business activity is envisaged in the Slovene economic system. The economic policies of Slovenia in the coming period should operate on the principles of a stabilisation of credit and monetary policies, still with relatively high real interest rates, and with tax and fiscal policies which allow only a minimum (1% GDP) budget deficit.

At the Crossroads of Three Cultures

The Freising manuscripts (9th c.) were the first writings in the Slovene language

The first Slovene translation of the Bible (1584) — The rich Baroque Seminary library in Ljubljana preserves some important written documents

Language and literature

The Reformation brought literacy and general culture to the Slovenes in the 16th century, and the appearance of the oldest Slovene literature shows a link with the great neighbouring cultures (German, Romance, Slavic). Manuscripts from Friesing in Germany, three manuscripts in the Latin alphabet in the Slavic dialect which was the forerunner of Slovene, are the oldest known writing. Made between 970 and 1000 AD, in them are inscribed the words: "Where our forebears without sin…"

The Slovenes obtained their first printed book in 1551 – "The Catechism" of Primož Trubar, and in 1584 the first translation into Slovene of the Bible, by Jurij Dalmatin, and a grammar by Adam Bohorič. The foundations were laid, and not even the counter-Reformation, which was charged with extirpating the seed of Protestantism, was able to destroy them.

Drama and poetry – if we discount popular creativity which had already provided some exceptional, primarily lyrical poetry – awoke at the turn of the

The Stična manuscript, 15th century, one of the oldest in Slovene

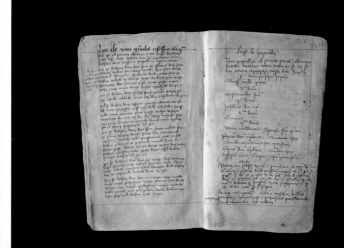

Birthplace of poet France Prešeren, in Vrba in Gorenjska

44 18th and 19th centuries. The poems of Valentin Vodnik and the plays of Anton T. Linhart express the libertarian spirit of the French Enlightenment and the French Revolution. The formal simplicity of their work, which is close to popular rhymes in theme and expression, is no accident: they knew that they were writing for the first literary public of their nation. The great educational reforms of the Austrian empress, Maria Theresa, and the mass literacy of the populations of these parts had begun in 1776. How much more surprising, therefore, was the maturity of the poet who came after them – France Prešeren. A lawyer and freethinker, a bohemian, an alcoholic and an eternally indomitable spirit, Prešeren brought to Slovene poetry all the principle classical poetic forms; he spiritually kindled the subalpine province with the fighting spirit of the European Romantics and thus, just as the great Romantics in other Slavic lands, articulated the national consciousness. A century and a half after its creation, his "Zdravljica" (The Toast) has become the national anthem of the Slovene state.

The writer, Ivan Cankar, and the poet, Oton Župančič, established the "Modern" trend in Slovene literature at the beginning of the century. Their esthetic criteria and political activities inspired the Slovenes prior to the creation of the state of Serbs, Croats and Slovenes

The nineteenth century, the great period of novels, provided the first Slovene example of this kind, with Josip Jurčič's "The Tenth Son". The model for this and other of Jurčič's tales (he also wrote short stories) were English historical novels, adapted to the environment in which they were created – dating from the time of the Turkish sieges, of the fate of people of originality and imagined erotic passions in a province where the sharp division between estate owners and cottagers forbade closer links. Jurčič was also the first Slovene journalist who, together with Fran Levstik, created the basis of domestic literary criticism. Long known only as a collector of popular wares but in reality a discerning observer and the most honest recorder of life in these parts, especially after the final appearance of diaries in the eighties of this century, Janez Trdina has also obtained his rightful place.

The generation of the Modern, which appeared at the turn of the twentieth century, brought the syndrome of "damned poets" since it began as a fellow

Dolenjska has provided a fair number of important writers: Trubar, Jurčič, Levstik, Trdina and others

traveller of European symbolism and decadence. It was later shown that the Slovene reaction of traditional Catholic conformity was exaggerated: Josip Murn Aleksandrov was a genuine poet, attached even to popular poetic tradition, which he was known to rework into sensitive modern poetic miniatures; during his short life, Dragotin Kette wrote with more cheerfulness and energy than all the previous Slovene poets; and Ivan Cankar and Oton Župančič became undisputed cultural and spiritual authorities, essentially influencing political life. Cankar, a master of symbolic sketches and somewhat Ibsenish tinged plays about the disintegration of provincial values at a time of industrialisation and the advance of capital, was throughout active as an enthusiastic essayist, and he propagated the idea of a Yugoslav state. Župančič, whose expressly modern approach to poetry and powerful poetic personality made him for many years the standard for other poets, also supported the

The Prekmurje lowlands are the setting for the novels of Miško Kranjec (1908–1983)

resistance movement from the start of the second world war and national uprising.

An unfinished first decade after the first world war was undoubtedly the time of Srečko Kosovel, a lyric poet, constructivist, apocalyptic herald of the end of Europe – a poet whose opus, in terms of volume and eruptive creative power and in its influence, which lasted for another fifty years, gives no hint that the author died only twenty years old. Between the wars, prose was dominated by social realism; Lovro Kuhar-Prežihov Voranc, Miško Kranjec and the somewhat gentler Ciril Kosmač were particularly outstanding. Ciril Kosmač reached his peak only after the war, with a shift to a more contemporary mode of narration; his story "Tantandruj" (Thatunthere) blurs the border between reality and fiction. The novel "Alamut" was written in the thirties, out of the main stream. Its author, Vladimir Bartol, a psychologist by training and a Nietzschean by conviction, did not live to see the rise, after some decades of being overlooked, of his story of an Islamic Empire in which

Srečko Kosovel, an exceptional visionary and contributor to the creation of the European avant-garde

Edvard Kocbek, poet and thinker, a central Slovene intellectual of the mid 20th century

the Emperor retained power by the skilful manipulation of his servants' pleasures. Alamut was only translated into all world languages half a century after its creation.

During the occupation, in 1941–45, the leadership of the resistance announced a so-called cultural silence, but nevertheless, an interesting poetry and prose production remains from this period which is sometimes breathtaking, more in the unified creative spirit of the nation than in the power of individual authors. However, there was some exceptional lyric poetry written at this time: the poems of Jože Udovič and Edvard Kocbek; as well as Karel Destovnik-Kajuh and France Balantič, one of whom was a partisan and the other a white guard, and the poetry of both was silenced too soon. The same could be said of the Expressionist poet, Miran Jarc.

The main figure of post-war literature was Edvard Kocbek. Not only because, soaked in Catholic mysticisn, he built his poetically very articulate world on more permanent foundations than those available to post-war materialism, but also because of his political conviction. At one time one of Tito's nomenclature, he became a dissident after a dispute at the start of the **47** fifties. His partisan diaries, essays, and personal integrity, made an indelible mark on the spiritual image of the nation.

Later post-war generations gradually turned away from realism and began to go their own ways. The most prominent of the poets are Janez Menart, Tone Pavček, Ivan Minatti, Ciril Zlobec, Tomaž Šalamun, Niko Grafenauer; and among the prose writers, Lojze Kovačič, Vladimir Kavčič, Pavle Zidar, Vitomil Zupan and Drago Jančar…

Theatre, film, radio and television

The history of Slovene National Theatre dates back to the time when Slovenia had Vienna as its capital, but its home was Ljubljana. Today, the Slovene state capital can be proud of the variety of theatres: drama, opera and ballet companies of the Slovene National Theatre, Ljubljana Municipal Theatre, Slovene Youth Theatre and a number of experimental theatres of which the best known abroad are troupes which use non-verbal means of expression,

The Slovenes are masters of the art of spectacle. Performance of Faust at Maribor theatre

mainly movement and dance. There are also drama, opera and ballet companies of the Slovene National Theatre in Maribor, noticeably flourishing recently, and professional theatres perform in Celje, Kranj (at the beginning of the century, it was a professional theatre seating 800), Nova Gorica and Trieste; the latter (in Italy) by international agreement which enables and guarantees the Slovene minority their own top quality artistic creativity. Amateur theatre activity is also widespread.

A number of full length movies are made each year in Slovenia, with different themes, from youth movies to genre attempts, though most of them are so-called author movies. Slovene radio and television supplements this production with original drama programmes. In addition to the national radio and television house, which transmits two television and three radio programmes, several local and regional stations have appeared in the aether recently. Private capital is also becoming more and more interested in the media.

Ana Monro Travelling Theatre, the challenge of alternative theatre

Music

There is documentary evidence that the Slovenes brought their own musical culture with them to their new homeland in the 6th century; they already had expressions like "pesem" and "peti" ("song" and "singing"), and from Christianisation (from the 8th century onwards), choral singing was nurtured. Medieval song was created between the 11th and 15th centuries. Monasteries, parish churches and schools looked after melodic and harmonic choral and liturgical singing. By the end of the middle ages, church music had reached a relatively high level and had developed the polyphony of the Europe of the time. Trubar's contemporary, Jakob Petelin-Gallus (1550–1591), whose nickname Carniolus testifies to his birth somewhere in Carniolia, was particularly notable.

The music of the late middle ages in Slovenia was linked to the modest

Music of Renaissance composer, Jakob Petelin Gallus-Carniolus. It is still not known from where exactly in Slovenia he came

circumstances in which the Slovene people and the few nobility lived; the more **49** able musicians went abroad. In the eighteenth century, the conditions for music had changed in important ways. No more Baroque, but Classicism and a turn to opera – the Slovenes were among the first to take it over from the Italians. The first Slovene opera was written at that time, Belin, by J. Zupan and F. A. Dev. In 1701, Ljubljana received its Academia Philharmonicorum, the forerunner of today's Philharmonia. The house was several times a short stop for important musicians – Beethoven, Mahler, Smetana. In the period of the Romantics (19th century), the most important representatives were Benjamin Ipavec, Fran Gerbič and Anton Foerster; Risto Savin best represents the new Romantics, and in the Modern flow of European music, the measure was set here after the first world war by Marij Kogoj and Slavko Osterc. Among the post-Romantics, mention should be made of Lucijan Marija Škerjanec.

This creativity was interrupted by the second world war, but this period of Slovene resistance – most of the important musicians took part in the resistance movement – fermented musical creativity with a new genuine self-awareness and modern national expression.

The Opera House in Ljubljana, one of two Slovene opera houses

Choirs are an unique juncture of folk and formal musical cultures. The annual meeting in Šentvid by Stična brings together several thousand singers

50   After 1945, most composers of the prewar generation continued their work but the intensive and fruitful Modernist efforts of the twenties and thirties were not renewed. Nevertheless, the post-war period can be said to have offered wide possibilities for multi-sided development enriched by contact with contemporary schools of musical creativity in Europe. This is confirmed by names like Primož Ramovš, Lojze Lebič, Jakob Jež, Vinko Globokar..., and is testified by the two opera ensembles (Ljubljana, Maribor), the two central symphonic orchestras (Slovene Philharmonic and RTV Slovenia) and a series of top creative musical artists, including Dubravka Tomšič, Marjana Lipovšek, Irena Grafenauer, the Slovene Octet and others.

    Choral singing among the Slovenes is really first class and popular. The meeting of choirs at Šentvid by Stična each year brings together several thousand singers of all possible choral forms. The event is social and spiritual at the same time, without awards but nevertheless not without the little competitive goad which has been raising the quality of the singing for more than a hundred years.

Laibach. They and other members of Neue Slowenische Kunst — the painting group Irwin and the theatre company Scipion Nasice — made the most astonishing breakthrough into the world by Slovene art

Representatives of alternative music and culture, groups like Laibach and Borghesia, which are among the most outstanding exemplars of their musical trends on the world stage, are certainly a specifically Slovene phenomenon. The first group in particular, within in the art movement, Neue Slowenische Kunst, marked a new artistic direction which has been followed in different forms by a great part of eastern Europe.

Visual arts

The most important Slovene fine art can be seen in national institutions such as the National Gallery and the Modern Gallery in Ljubljana, in numerous smaller galleries and salons throughout Slovenia, and three Forma Viva: at Seča by Portorož, for stone sculpture; Kostanjevica by Krka, for wood; and Ravne na Koroškem, for iron. Above all, however, the fine arts mark the environment wherever one goes. Painter and sculptor have been our constant

Janez of Kastav: The Dance of Death. A variant of a famous motif in Hrastovlje

attendant; from anonymous church painters to members of the Radgona school (Janez Aquila); from the Dance of Death in Hrastovlje church, by Janez of Kastav above Rijeka, to the mighty frescoes of the Slovene compatriot from Austrian Carinthia, Valantin Oman; from Romantic landscape painters of Karinger's reputation to the quatro of Impressionists (Jakopič, Sternen, Jama, Grohar). These four, who were a part of the Modern movement, contributed, together with the great name of Ažbe and his Munich school, one of the biggest steps forward in European art and remain today among the most important representatives of Slovene art.

Continuity in this field is also assured with the activities in Ljubljana of the Academy of Fine Arts. Slovene painters are keeping pace with world creativity, as are sculptors, successors to the traditions of Berneker, Zajc, Kalin, Savinšek and many others. All have made their mark on this land, as have Fabiani and

Anton Karinger: Triglav from Bohinj – Rihard Jakopič: Sipina (below)

Janez Boljka: Bull, bronze

Janez Bernik: Note 965/989, graphic

Plečnik, architects whose heirs have designed the contemporary Slovene space.

An International Graphics Biennial was initiated in 1955 under the auspices of the Modern Gallery, expanding in 1987 to an international graphic arts centre. In addition to architecture, Slovene design has also entered the world in ways which a foreigner might meet without being aware. There are well known chairs designed by Niko Kralj, or you may be phoning from an Iskra telephone, which received many design awards; or at least from its Far East copy. The international ICSID congress held in Ljubljana in May 1992 was also recognition of achievements in the field of design; and fashion in Slovenia has provided plenty of new approaches to give variety to the Slovene lifestyle.

Academy, university, education

Any discussion on Slovene culture must take account of such important institutions as the Slovene Academy of Sciences and Arts and the University.

The most important artistic heritage is preserved in the National Gallery in Ljubljana

The University is officially older since, although not complete, it started work after the first world war (1919). The Academy was founded just prior to the second world war (1938) but has deep roots reaching back to the 17th century; to the Academia Operosorum, which can be taken as the precursor of our main institution of science and arts. Other than the Academy, Ljubljana University was our only top educational institution for the entire period up to the second world war and for long years after it (until the founding of the University of Maribor).

There is, of course, a long way to the universities through primary and secondary education. This is done by young Slovenes in twelve years. Primary school is compulsory and lasts eight years. Secondary schools are usually four years. Some of them are oriented to particular professions, others (gymnasiums) are primarily preparation for higher education. Public education is in

The "old" University building in Ljubljana

54 principle free and, therefore, for everyone, but possibilities for private schools are now opening up.

Science

The first Slovene intellectuals who might be called scholars appeared in the 12th century, and humanists of Slovene origin appeared between the 15th and 17th centuries, working in various European universities. The first really wellknown Slovene scientist, however, was the social historian, Janez Vajkard Valvasor (1641–1693), a member of the British Royal Society. In 1689, he published in three thousand five hundred pages, a richly illustrated work, "In Praise of the Duchy of Carniola", which thoroughly presented a central part of Slovenia to Europe.

In the middle of the 17th century, Jesuits began to introduce high school studies. The first scientific academy operated in Ljubljana in the period from 1693 to 1725. In 1762 – almost one hundred years before Pasteur – the physician Marko Plenčič recognised the cause of contagious diseases as being

The National and University Library holds around 2,000,000 bibliographical units. The building, the work of architect Jože Plečnik, is also an exceptional architectural monument

Rudi Španzel: Portraits for the Slovene
tolar of Slovene personalities
from culture and history

Top to bottom:

Primož Trubar and Jakob Gallus

Janez Vajkard Valvasor and Jurij Vega

France Prešeren and Rihard Jakopič

Jože Plečnik

micro-organisms. An Enlightenment circle around Baron Žiga Zois was very active at the end of the 18th and start of the 19th century. The mathematician, Jurij Vega, then completed logarithms which were in widespread use for two hundred years until the appearance of the computer. In 1819, Jernej Kopitar, one of the greatist Slavists of all time, wrote the first scientific grammer of the Slovene language and his work was continued by Fran Miklošič. The greatest Slovene physicist, Jožef Stefan, discovered the law of heat radiation in 1879. Soon after the earthquake in 1895, Ljubljana obtained the most advanced seismological station in Europe.

In 1906, Slovene mathematician, Josip Plemelj, solved Rieman's problem, which was considered unsolvable, and three years later, Edvard Rusjan made the first flight with his motor plane. In the first years of the Slovene university, mathematician Josip Plemelj, architect Jože Plečnik, electronic expert of international repute Milan Vidmar, chemist Maks Samec and other scientists

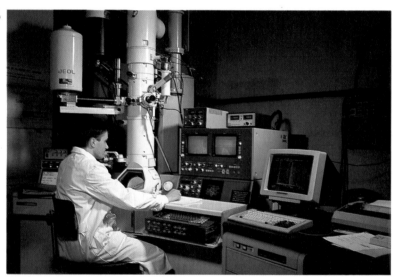

Jožef Stefan Institute, the central research foundation. Work with high definition electron microscope

worked there. In 1923, Ljubljana born Friderik Pregl received the Nobel prize for the introduction of organic chemical micro-analysis. A little later, engineer Herman Potočnik-Noordung wrote one of the basic astronautics pioneer works. In the mid thirties, a consistent scientific approach replaced empirical technical thinking in Slovenia, and mechanic and constructor Anton Kuhelj had a decisive role in this process.

After the second world war, a number of basic institutes were established in Slovenia: physics, chemistry, electrotechnical and others. The Physics Institute, named after Jožef Stefan, has become Slovenia's largest research institute, with around 500 scientists. Its founder and first head, physicist Anton Peterlin, went abroad in 1960 and became one of the top scientists for large molecules and polymerisation. An accelerated drain of Slovene brains started in this year; on a rough estimate, at least half of the most important Slovene scientists are

1st and 2nd century Roman tombs in Šempeter by Žalec

working abroad, and those at home are also involved in international links. **57**
Many of them are among leading world scientists in their fields.

In 1975, the second Slovene university was founded in Maribor and in Ljubljana, the modern University Clinical Centre was opened. In the same year, physicist Bogdan Povh became director of the Max Plank institute for nuclear research in Heidelberg.

Historical Monuments

Traces of European civilisation on Slovene soil date to when man made his first sewing needle in a cave under Olševa. In the 7th century BC, during the Hallstatt era, there were castle dwellers in Šentvid by Stična. They carried bronze helmets from there to Vače and Novo mesto, and made ornamented metal situlae. The figurines and rich reliefs on the situlae, interweaving scenes from real life and myth, are echoes of a time and people on the artery between the Bavarian plains and the Adriatic and they are unique in Europe.

The Celts came, followed by the Romans. In addition to great cities,

Excavated pagan castle in Vranje by Sevnica. The ruins of the largest early Christian centre in the Alps and along the Danube

Poetovio, Celeia, Emona, they built a series of fortifications and roads. They erected villas ornamented with beautiful mosaics. They built temples to various gods and adorned them with stone ornamentation. Slovenia, a meeting point of influences, was a place of cults to Mithras, Hercules and Jupiter. The dead were given tombs such as may be seen today in Šempeter. The Emonan, the statue to a former citizen, for several decades guarded the northern gates to the city of former Ljubljana. The military organisation of the land was effected through the castrum. Slovene lands became the outer ramparts of central European territory.

The great Roman empire fell in the 5th century, the people turned to new intercessors and fell back to the less accessible hills. Various tribes governed after the Huns; tangible traces have been left of the Langobardi. Roman civilisation vegetated in fragments along the Adriatic, from Poreč to Aquilea and Venice.

In the 7th century, the Slavs finally dominated the land between the Drava and the Adriatic. Christianity was reawakened among them in the late middle ages. The first churches were clumsy single nave chapels, narrow, with modest gable roofs, such as still stand on Holy mountains. The defence accommodation towers of the first landowners were similarly angular. The Roman palaces had had to have thick walls, with occasional slit windows which were more lines for shooting than sources of light.

Monks came to the abandoned land on the edge of Europe, and with them in the 12th century, a French seminarian, Michael, who founded a Cistercian monastery in Stična, in the midst of the broad hills and forests. Many "newcomers" came among the natives and stayed. After the monasteries in Stična and Gornji Grad, came further monasteries of different orders; in Konstanjevica, Pleterje and, in 1260, in Bistra. All were overshadowed by elegant and aristocratic Žiče, built after 1165. With its slender Gothic form, the ruins are still today an important part of the European heritage of the art of building.

Ljubljana is first mentioned in 1144. Noblemen and worthy urban gentlefolk wanted something new. At that time, the Franciscan monks and their young brethren had brought a new pointed form with large windows and

12th century Romanesque rotunda in Selo (Prekmurje)

The oldest Slovene monastery, Stična, founded in 1135 and Carthusian Pleterje from the early 15th century (below)

ribbed long choirs. At Ptujska gora after 1398, the slender form was rewoven and became a hall, decorated with high quality sculpture. More modest communities built single nave churches of which at least the presbytery was vaulted. The insides of these churches, and frequently the outsides too, were ablaze with rainbow colours; Carnolian Presbytery was created, costly Suhe, Mače, Mirna and Bločice. The Dance of Death, the impressive fresco in the church at Hrastovlje, announced a new era.

In the 15th and 16th centuries, the Turks and other adversities made the population susceptible. They listened eagerly to the Protestant preachers. There was no enthusiasm here for building new shrines; Trubar thundered from the pulpit against pomp and costly imagery. New buildings, such as the church of St. Peter in Dvor near Polhov Gradec, were rare; farmers built defensive camps, nobles stout ramparts. In 1511, a serious earthquake shook

Predjamski grad by Postojna, 16th century, full of legend

60 Slovenia. Builders from Friuli, in Italy, assisted in the rebuilding and brought Renaissance elements to castles and other buildings. Castles were given new towers, arcaded courtyards and lower battlements. Castle chapels and great halls were decorated.

Building on Slovene lands flourished. The entire landscape became a set (this was the period of Molliere and Mozart) and Slovenia opened itself to the Baroque. The very name of Sladka gora (Sweet mountain) testifies to its form and content. Tunjice, protected by towers and stressed with a cupola, is a reflection of Roman and Ljubljana churches against a backdrop of mountains. Nobles from Dornava to Planina and Dol built manor houses with landscaped parks; they walked among fountains and statuary. Especially in the first half of the 18th century, Slovene towns confidently invited the greatest architects of the Baroque: Andrea Pozzi, Paccassi, Giorgio Massari. They in turn trained domestic masters, Gregor Maček, Jožef Hofer and Jožef Fuchs. The interiors of places of worship had already been made magnificent with golden altars, to which was added the stone lacework of sculptor Francesco Robba and his contempories. They commissioned paintings from the then best

Church of the Holy Spirit in Bohinj. Characteristic Alpine church today also host performances of the Ljubljana Summer Festival

known artists, from Fortunat Bergant to Anton Cebej, Frančišek Jelovšek and Valentin Metzinger. Bergant left his Stations of the Cross in the very church which Candido Zulliani had reconstructed for the builder Michael.

Stucco work moved from the halls of castles to the corridors, castle frescoes imitated the vivacity of Versailles. Religious motifs were replaced by Hercules and the gods of Olympus. Opulence came to Dornava, Brežice and Slovenska Bistrica.

The French Revolution in 1789 gave birth to a new, more strictly classical form. Temple frontages and Classical columns were given to Ljubljana Kasino, Coconi's Souvan house, the facade of Nobil's church of St. Peter in Piran or Pertsch's renovated health spa of Rogaška Slatina. These lands were briefly the Illyrian provinces, before their fate was decided by rulers at the Congress of the Holy Alliance in Ljubljana in 1821. Congress square is a reminder of this and it extended over Zvezda park to Latterman avenue. The rigid Austro-Hunga-

Franc Jelovšek: The Holy Family (1734). Tramp d'oeil work by Baroque masters in St. Peter's church (Ljubljana) — Dornava castle near Ptuj. Formerly one of the finest Baroque manor houses and parks in these parts (right)

rian framework introduced the historically imitative palaces of Frederik Schmidt and his contemporaries.

In April 1895, an earthquake again shook Ljubljana and many old houses were destroyed. They were replaced by buildings erected in the spirit of the Vienna Secession, which quickly became fashionable throughout Slovenia. Czech and German artists were joined by Max Fabiani, born on the Karst. National consciousness sprouted alongside proud memorials to native poets: Valentin Vodnik and France Prešeren and the father of the Slovene language, Primož Trubar.

When the new state was born in 1919, Jože Plečnik (1872–1957) returned to the Slovene capital. In echo of Vienna and Prague examples, the architect

Jože Plečnik: St. Michael on the Marsh near Ljubljana

62 created a new synthesis of northern elements and the Mediterranean spirit. He transformed the ambient beside the Ljubljanica, built the University library and erected church buildings which found echoes as far away as Bogojina.

After victory in the second world war, the development of forms of pathos was stressed. The people's wounds demanded memorials, too many memorials. They sprang up in the middle of the countryside as much as in urban settlements. However, architecture and the memorials remained on a typical Slovene miniature scale until the sixties, which brought the skyscraper from the world. The new Revolution Square, the work of architect Edo Ravnikar, has experienced various schools with the gradual building of towers, a department store and the Congress centre and has retained all the marks of time. The architect, Marko Mušič, has shown a different approach, again with church building, in the Ljubljana suburb of Dravlje.

HABITS AND CUSTOMS

Slovenia's cultural variety is certainly one of its major attractions, the confluence of Alpine, coastal and lowland cultures, with their own approaches to building, nutrition and the economy, their own manners and customs, and traditions of song and artistic creation. So a real motley tapestry of cultural forms emerged in this part of the world, from which heritage contemporary lifestyle has sprung.

The countryside has lost its former originality with modern organisation and ill-considered tailor-made building, but these have not destroyed its spirit completely. The Karst villages, and isolated farms in the mountains and rural village housing in north-east Slovenia, are outstanding examples; and there are many variations among outbuildings. The Slovene hayrack, a structure for drying and storing hay and other crops, is unknown elsewhere. It emerged over the course of history through the interweaving of all three cultures on this space and it not only gives a significant character to the cultural landscape but is also a good example – if not a monument – to the interweaving of the aesthetic and functional in the life of the Slovenes.

Nutrition

If there is anything in the slogan that "Man is what he eats" (Homo est, quid edit) then the variety of food tells a lot about the Slovenes, their needs, manners and customs, lifestyle – from porridge or bread based food in the north-east of Slovenia to the Mediterranean diet of coastal parts, an interesting combination of vegetable dishes supplemented by pršut – an air dried ham – and the famous Teran wine whose very name hints at its earthy quality. Pork dishes are a significant culinary item and the killing of the pig was always an important family occasion. Typical folk dishes such as various traditional roll cakes, "gibanica" (layer cake) and dishes from buckwheat, are again appearing on the menues of better restaurants. The choice of drinks is also very wide, from fruit juices and fruit brandies to top quality wines. Of the wines, teran from the Karst, "cviček" from Dolenjska, and archive wines from Štajerska, are worth special mention.

The most characteristic Slovene dishes were those from buckwheat

The village of Podkoren has retained the typical Alpine architecture: solid buildings with wood shingles covering the roofs

Hay barns in Studor, an autochtonous expression of vernacular construction
Woodcraft from Ribnica is an example of the high development of cottage crafts

Masters built churches, popular artists plague signs and signposts (below)
Transition from popular to high art. The wrought dragon has its roots in Kropa

Wedding with a touch of tradition. The family is still very high on the scale of Slovene values

The charms of craft

A wealth of cottage and artisan crafts has been preserved and many have even recently been reviving. Many villages and towns have their own potters, wickermakers, blacksmiths, woodsmiths and other artisans who continue the craft tradition, and seek new solutions in modern design. The Slovene archetype in this field are makers of woodware – woodsmiths who obtained permission from the German Emperor five hundred years ago (1492) to trade freely in their products. Over the centuries, they paved trade routes through a considerable part of Europe, to the coast of Asia Minor, and the Mediterranean to Africa and even to India.

Old festivals in new dress

The Slovenes have many different festivals through the course of the year. Much of the heritage has been preserved in the context of different popular (tourist) events, though of course, the nucleus of customs is still bound to celebration in the family circle. Individual days in spring are celebrated, then harvest and grape picking, different customs are connected with Martinmas,

Popular craft achieved its peak in wood and clay

Kurents, the most characteristic and best known of the Slovene Pust figures, come from Ptujsko polje. Driving away evil spirits and heralding spring

66 Pust (coinciding with Shrove Tuesday), Christmas and Easter. At the time of Pust, numerous costumed groups and individual characters appear in the Slovene countryside, of which the most famous manifestation is the masque of the Kurent in Markovci and nearby villages on Ptujsko polje. Christmas and Easter retain many local particularities. The Easter painting of eggs in Bela Krajina and in Prekmurje has achieved the level of real folk art.

The variety and heterogeneity of Slovene culture and lifestyle are supplemented by the artistic heritage in churches, castles, old towns and village centres, and of course in galleries and museums. There is one further speciality which deserves attention: the painted frontispanels of beehives. They are real galleries of popular life, religious performances, as well as witty comment on human character, foibles, values and ethical norms. The painting of beehives emerged as a special branch of folk art in the second half of the 18th century and it reached its peak in the 19th century.

The Vienna court apiarist, the Slovene Anton Janša, at the end of the 18th century cultivated an autochtonous species of Carnolian bee. Beehive at Muljava

The baker's art and popular ornament – walnut roll and painted eggs from Bela krajina

Beltinci band, a popular folk band from Prekmurje

Slovene Towns

68 Ljubljana, Capital city (population 276,200)

The capital of Slovenia may well seduce you after your first walk through the old town centre, with its Renaissance, Baroque and Secession facades, decorated portals and vaulted atriums. It nestles between the castle hill and the Ljubljanica river. Its Baroque churches and palaces are among the most beautiful examples of their kind in Central Europe. A fine vista opens over the city from the castle (foundations from the 9th century, present form from the 16th century), which is currently undergoing total renovation. Ljubljana has been growing fast since the second world war and today has almost 300,000 inhabitants.

Far beyond the last tower blocks rise the hills which enclose Ljubljana basin to the north; to the south is marshland, the Barje. Remains of pile dwellings have been found on the Barje which can now be viewed in museums. Traces of the past are also visible in the heart of the town: houses and defensive moats, walls, towers, sculptures and the cool buildings of the ancient former town of Emona, all of which testify to a highly developed civilisation even in the far past. The migration of nations brought its own civilisation, various armies

Tromostovje, the Three Bridges, a unique link of the citadel with the rest of the city

The heart of Ljubljana is mostly Baroque

penetrated and retreated through the "Ljubljana Gate". This position at a crossroads greatly affected the development of the town and it was often an important administrative and cultural centre.

Ljubljana is mentioned for the first time as Leybach in 1144 and then in 1146 as Luwigana, with the Town and Old squares below the castle, and New square evolving later, separated from the start by the Ljubljanica river. There was lively traffic on the Ljubljanica in the past, including a steamboat from Vrhnika to the landing at Breg. Traffic diminished when Ljubljana got a railway in the middle of last century.

The busiest and best known of the bridges over the river is Tromostovje (Three Bridges), conceived by architect Jože Plečnik in the thirties, such that it retained its former stone bridge to which he added two footbridges. Nearby Zmajski most (Dragon bridge) is decorated with dragons, the symbol of

Dragon, symbol of Ljubljana
The Town Hall, with Robba's Fountain

Prešeren square by Tromostovje, in the centre of Ljubljana

Ljubljana ever since one of the dragons found itself on the city coat-of-arms a few centuries ago. Čevljarski most (Cobbler's bridge) and many other buildings which have given character to the city were erected to Plečnik's plans. The master had planned a Slovene parliament and wanted to turn Ljubljana castle into a Slovene Acropolis. The National and University Library, the open market by the Ljubljanica, Žale cemetery, the Garden of All Saints, the adaptation of Križanke for the summer theatre, the churches of St. Francis in Šiška and St. Michael on the Marsh and the central stadium are undoubtedly among his masterpieces. A walk through Plečnik's Ljubljana is not just a view of the opus of a great artist but also a pilgrimage through all the worthwhile parts of the town. In addition to Jože Plečnik, of Modern architects mention should be made also of Max Fabiani, who conceived one of the most beautiful Secession parks in the city centre – Slovene park in front of the Palace of Justice – and other Secession buildings at the sides of the park put up after the earthquake at the end of the last century.

In the thirties, Ljubljana gained its first skyscraper, which has been overtaken by some later buildings, though Ljubljana has not experienced any excessive growth in height. The city extended breadthwise along all the main traffic roads running towards the centre. A new city business and cultural centre emerged in the seventies and a second business trade centre has developed in the region of Ajdovščina square, to the plans of the architect Janez Lajovic and his associates.

The former main post office mid-way between Tivoli park and the town hall is still the central point of Ljubljana. There is a fine view from here towards Tivoli castle, where there is now an international graphic arts centre.

Plan of the centre of Ljubljana

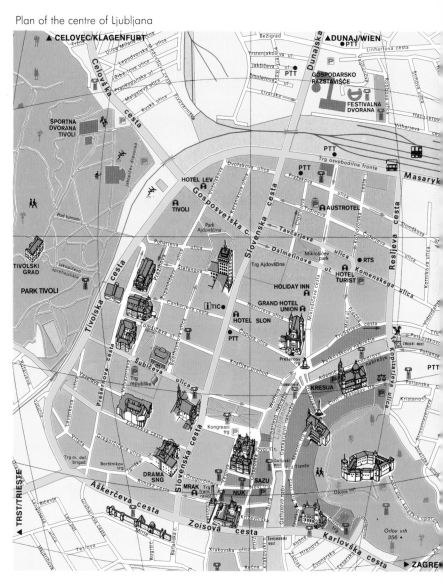

Summer in old Ljubljana

There are several other castles in addition to this one and the castle on the hill: Cekin and Fužine castle housing two of the numerous museums, and a number of others, such as Rakovnik and Kodeljevo, which need restoration and to be given an appropriate content.

Ljubljana has more churches than castles. The Baroque church of St. Peter near the University Clinical Centre is the oldest Ljubljana parish church; the new church of the Incarnation of Christ, in Dravlje, by the old church of St. Rok is the most modern. Peace between the Habsburgs and the Venetian Republic was concluded in the distant past in front of St. Bartholomew's old church in Šiška. The cathedral church of St. Nicholas, restored in Baroque, has a beautiful Pieta from the fifteenth century (replaced by a copy) in a niche in the exterior wall and in the interior, there is a real exhibition of Ljubljana sculptors' workshop, which is continued in the church of St. James in old

Šuštarski most, the Cobbler's bridge; yet another of Plečnik's bridges across the Ljubljanica

Ljubljana and in the mighty Baroque church of the Holy Trinity (Ursuline church) on the edge of Congress square, named after the Congress of the Holy Alliance in 1821, when there was the meeting of the Austrian Emperor, the Russian Czar and the Neapolitan King and other important persons in the city. The steps of the Franciscan church which looks over Tromostovje is a popular place for youth to sit. Trnovo church is in the immediate vicinity of the architectural museum set up in the house of architect Jože Plečnik.

Ljubljana also has several noble palaces: the County House, now the University building, the Neo-renaissance government building, Stiški dvorec, the Bishop's palace. The historical archives of Slovenia are kept in Grubar palace, which was built by Gabrijel Gruber, who also helped in producing plans for the drainage of Ljubljana Marsh and for the channel which was named after him. The town hall under the hill in the old town has a mighty facade and a courtyard decorated with graffiti. The facade was formerly ornamented with statues of Adam and Eve. They are now moved to the Cultural and Information Centre in Križanke which, in addition to the Tourist Information Centre, provides useful information. Robba's Fountain of the

The southern part of the Slovene capital opens onto the Barje (marsh), where the first settlements 4,000 years ago were on stilts

Cankarjev dom, congress and cultural centre

74 Three Carniolian Rivers stands in front of the town hall and nicely rounds off the Baroque appearance of Mestni trg, the town square.

Cultural life in Ljubljana is so plentiful that the city is competing for the title of Cultural Capital of Europe in 1995. Events and exhibitions enliven city life throughout the year; most of them are in Križanke − especially during the summer festival − and in Cankarjev dom. Present culture is interwoven with reminders of the cultural past: in front of the entrance to the cultural centre, there is a monument to the greatest Slovene writer, Ivan Cankar; a monument to the "father of the nation", the poet Dr. France Prešeren, stands in Prešeren square in front of the Franciscan church; the sculpture of Valentin Vodnik faces away from the open market; a bust of painter Rihard Jakopič stands in front of the gallery which bears his name; and linguist Fran Miklošič has been given his place in Slovene park.

Ljubljana citizens used to enjoy coffee houses − "kavarne". These have recently been transformed and have lost their former charm. They are also in strong competition with the small coffee bars which have sprouted like mushrooms after rain and are most numerous in the old town, where there are

The castle, slowly but surely being given a new appearance. The Philharmonia below

Tivoli Park. Plečnik's promenade, the International Graphic Art Centre behind
Panorama of the new part of Ljubljana

Youth on the street of Ljubljana

many small galleries and private shops, too. The old town is liveliest in summer, with numerous events in the atriums and squares.

The main city park, Tivoli, is the green lungs of the city; there are several sports courts and Tivoli sports hall. Rožnik and Šišenski hrib are large green areas available for sports and walking enthusiasts, and the green belts along the Ljubljanica and the Sava rivers in the north part of Ljubljana could be considered nature reserves. There is a more than 30 kilometres long circular avenue laid out around Ljubljana, where barbed wire ringed the city during the second world war.

There was a time when the city was called "white" Ljubljana. Today, this whiteness is turning grey from exhaust fumes. It is lauded in song as a long village, which it is no longer. Today, it is a University city with eleven faculties and three academies and with the ambition of becoming a tourist and congress city at the European crossroads. Nevertheless, the traveller will find in it a unique combination of a tranquil and capital city which is bubbling with the spiritual energy of the nation.

Maribor (population 108,100)

Maribor is the second largest city in Slovenia. Its foundation is linked with the important fortress − castle − on the hill known as the Pyramid. The castle was called Marchbruch, or castle in the Marches, and the town with the same name emerged later below it. It developed along the river Drava and obtained town rights in 1254.

The town was initially artisan based, but trade also later developed. It was surrounded until the eighteenth century by a wall with inbuilt defense towers. Four are still preserved: Vodni stolp (water tower), where there is now a wine cellar, Sodni stolp (justice tower) , Celigijev stolp (Celigi's tower) and Židovski

Lent, former Maribor landing on the banks of the Drava

Main square of Maribor, with plague sign. Mary's Column with the six statuettes was erected in 1743

78 stolp (Jewish tower). There was a Jewish quarter around the last until the end of the fifteenth century. The synagogue was preserved, and later transformed into the Church of All Saints. This quarter of the city – locally known as Lent and for some time called Venice on the Drava – extends into the water where there was once a jetty at which rafts and cargo boats called. Lent, although not fully renovated, is becoming one of the most attractive parts of Maribor. The oldest vine (400 years!) in Europe grows in front of the pub at Vojašniška ulica 8. It still gives sixty litres of wine annually.

Maribor had at one time three castles. The first two no longer exist and the third, which has a 15th century late Gothic foundation, today houses the extensive collections of the regional museum. The most architecturally interesting parts of the castle are Loretan chapel, the great hall with its rich stucco work and paintings, and the late Baroque staircase. In front of the castle is the castle square, with a 17th century Florian pillar which was renovated and reerected a few years ago. On the other large square, named after Bishop Anton Martin Slomšek, who transferred the seat of the Laventine bishopric – is a Gothic light pillar from 1517. It used to stand in the city cemetery,

Baroque treasure still preserved: renovated building and Angel of grapes by Joseph Straub

Old and new: The oldest vine in Europe and the modern bus station

The Drava. The river which sets the seal for the whole town

which no longer exists. The Cathedral of John the Baptist, which contains a valuable Gothic stone sculpture, is lined with many tombs and Baroque fittings.

In Glavni trg, Main square, the oldest part of the city and its backbone, the eye lights first on a beautifully renovated, richly decorated Baroque plague sign from 1743. It appears in the middle of the square like an altar, with six statues surrounding the Column to Mary. Behind it is Baroque Aloysius' church and the former town hall, today an art gallery, with a stone balcony on which the city coat of arms is clearly visible. The coat of arms has, in addition to the town wall, open city gates with doves above.

Maribor was still considered a very proletarian and industrial city up to the fifties, but today it has expanded and become more middle class. There are new bridges over the Drava, and a glittering Post-modern bus station in the

Celje, strong Slovene industrial centre

centre of the city. The technical and economics faculties of the University of Maribor are also housed in new buildings in the centre, as is the university library.

Celje (population 41,300)

Celje has several times played an important historical role. In Roman times, Celeia flourished and earned recognition as "Troia secunda" – a second Troy. It gained importance beyond that of other Slovene towns in the 14th and 15th centuries, too, under the Counts and Dukes of Celje, who were connected with ruling families throughout Europe and reached quite high on the ladder of power, simultaneously obtaining considerable estates. The end of the Dukes of Celje closed a great chapter in the history of these parts.

Testimony of them abounds in books, monuments and museums. The regional museum is set up in the old 16th century County House, which is the most beautiful Renaissance building in Celje, with its oldest part leaning against the city wall. The ceilings in the great hall on the first floor are among the best Renaissance paintings in Slovenia. The Abbey church is considered by

Celje dom in the centre of the town (left) – The painted Renaissance ceiling in Celje old County House (right)

professionals to be among the oldest building in Celje, an originally Romanesque architectural monument restored in the 18th century. Its bell-tower rises above the roofs of the old town core. Many of the older houses have recently been restored, bringing out their original form. The embankments of the Savinja are well laid out and ideal for walks.

The best view of Celje is from old Celje castle hill. There is a viewing platform on top of the tower, which has two and a half metre thick walls. The castle is mainly in ruins, though conservationists are trying to restore as much as possible. Recent investigation of Celje's lower castle has revealed Romanesque and Gothic structural elements.

Kranj (population 37,300)

In the 11th century, Kranj, then known as Chreina, was the seat of the border counts. It gained town rights in the 13th century at the latest, and gave its

Kranj: market and industrial town on the way from Ljubljana towards Austria

name to the province of Carnolia. Today it is the fourth largest town in Slovenia and the county town of Gorenjska, at whose geographic centre it lies. The medieval part of Kranj spreads between the Sava and Kokra rivers, around the parish church of St. Kancian, the most important monument of Gothic architecture in Gorenjska. The new part, Zlato polje and Planina, is on a plain on the other side of the rivers.

The town hall on the former Kranj market square is outstanding in its diversity, with late Gothic columned vestibule and Classical columned porch. It contains the Gorenjska museum, a collection of the work of the Slovene sculptor, Lojze Dolinar, and an exhibition of folk art in Gorenjska. The house of the Slovene poet, France Prešeren, is only a few steps away and contains a memorial collection, with a gallery on the ground floor and in the cellar.

The people of Kranj have erected a monument to Prešeren on the square by the church of St. Kancian, where the building housing Kranj theatre has

Old part of Kranj with Storžič dominating the background

arcades by architect Jože Plečnik. Plečnik's architectural signature is also visible by the presbytery of the Church of the Rosary in Kranj. Prešeren's grove, a living memorial to the poet, has been set up the memorial park, an old Kranj cemetery in which the poet, Simon Jenko, is also buried.

Koper (population 25,300)

Koper lies along the short Slovene coast, and is the largest coastal town and the Slovene window on the world. Despite industrial growth, the town has preserved the old core untouched. It occupies an island close to the shore which has been variously called Kozji otok (Goat's island), Justinian town and by the Slovenes, Koper.

The town has been linked to the mainland since 1825. The later part of the town has an entirely different image, that of a modern town with high density

Koper is the heart of the Slovene coast and the only Slovene port

15th century Venetian Loggia in the heart of old Koper. Ships still sail to Venice from the very pretty coastal town

apartment blocks, contrasting with the typical coastal town appearance of the "island" part. There are clear Italian architectural influences, which is hardly surprising since Koper had an important position within the Venetian Republic.

There are numerous architectural monuments in this part of the town – from the Rotunda, with its typical Romanesque exterior, to the Praetorian Palace in the central square which has its rich architectural history inscribed on the facade, supplemented with the town's coat of arms and busts of Koper's important citizens with epitaphs; from Almerigogna palace, which is among the most magnificent Venetian Gothic palaces in Koper, to the Loggia, which has preserved the charm and character of its 15th century origin, and the cathedral (the seat of the Bishopric) with the sarcophagus of St. Nazarus and paintings by Vittorio Carpacci; from Belgramoni-Tacco palace, which houses the regional museum, to the da Ponte fountain, which obtained its present form in 1666 but had been mentioned two centuries earlier.

Piran (population 4,800)

Piran is the birthplace of the famous violinist and composer, Giuseppe Tartini, the bronze gentleman with a violin on the pedestal in the middle of the main square. The tomb of the Tartini family is in the church of St. Francis. There are several churches in Piran, the most prominent being the Renaissance-Baroque parish church of St. George, with a high lookout tower and Baptistry on a hill, from where there is a fine view to the sea over the roofs of the town's houses.

Piran is clustered on a narrow peninsular between Strunjan and Piran Bay and so the houses are compressed, the streets are narrow and there are historical gems at every step: the 17th century town gate of St. George; the 15th century building known as the Venetian, one of the most charming

Guiseppe Tartini, the famous composer (1692–1770), was born in Piran

Piran, the prettiest town on the coast

examples of Gothic architecture in Slovenia; "hanging houses" in the web of **85** narrow, winding small streets which form the characteristic architectural motif of Piran; the vaulted passages and arcaded courtyards of the 17th century Franciscan monastery; 15th century stone flagstaffs; Dolfin's, Milje's, the Cathedral and Central gates in the wall, which is still visible in parts, etc. All these pearls are bound into the unity of Piran, a first class monument.

Idrija (population 6,200)

Idrija is famous for lacework, "žlikrofi" (Idrijan style ravioli), for the scientists which helped gain it a reputation as the Slovene Athens of natural history and, of course, for the mercury which was drawn from the bowels of Idrija and gave the men their livelihood. The women, though, were mistresses of lacemaking. The first document on lacemaking in Idrija dates from 1696; the craft was very widespread in this region until the 19th century and is still actively practised today. There are beautiful examples in the museum collection in Idrija castle, built in 1533, after the mine administration building and the mercury warehouse. The collection of minerals in the museum is also exceptional.

Idrija was the third largest mercury mine in the world. Only the richly laid-out mining museum remains

Lacemaker's art, carried on in Idrija by the miner's wives, has developed its own patterns and still has a future

86   The discovery of mercury ore at the end of the 15th century gave birth of Idrija, which has already celebrated its 500th anniversary. It developed not just as a mining town, but an educational and cultural centre, with public, lacemaking and forestry schools, augmented by other schools in this century. Idrija mine, along with Spanish Almadena, was the largest mercury mine in Europe and it has had its ups and downs. Nevertheless, it has given its seal to the town. The old miners' houses and the fittings and building of the 1768 mine theatre, are still standing.

Škofja Loka (population 12,400)

In 1973, Škofja Loka celebrated 1000 years from the date when the Freising bishops established their administrative estates, which they managed for a full 830 years. A lot had changed in this time in the settlement which nestled into the hillside in three storeys above the confluence of the two Sora rivers, and got its name from the grassland along the water (loka=water meadows, škof =bishop). In 1314, the town was surrounded by a wall through which there were five gates protected with guard towers.

Škofja Loka, more than a millenium of history

Škofja Loka castle with interesting museum

The appearance of the old town core is mainly from the early 16th century, **87** the densely packed houses being partially enclosed by a wall. The narrow streets lead to more spacious Mestni trg, at the start of which is Homan's house with painted facade. A number of Škofja Loka houses had such facades, and the town was also referred to as "Painted" Loka. Mestni trg is also graced by a Baroque shrine to Mary from 1751, and a fountain with the town's coat of arms. Not far away is St. James parish church, slightly further the Capuchin church and monastery containing a valuable library. The new residential area, called the "New World", stretches out behind the monastery, below Lubnik mountain.

Loka castle is like a crown above the town, with extensive castle gardens in which occasional theatre performances are held and there is an outside museum. Loka museum is within the castle.

Radovljica (population 6,200)

This compact monument to urban architecture perches on an outcrop between the Sava and Suha rivers. It was first mentioned in documents in 1169, as

Radovljica, a town built on a high outcrop above the Sava river

Ratmansdorf, and in 1337 as a market town. The main square is now named after Anton Tomaž Linhart, the father of Slovene drama, born here in 1756. There are some beautiful examples of 16th and 17th century urban architecture in the square, the houses of Šivic and Koman being especially fine. The castle building occupies almost a quarter of the entire circumference of the square. It contains cultural institutions and the Museum of Apiculture, with collections which testify to the old tradition of apiculture and its Slovene particularities. The manor park attached to the castle was one of the finest examples of Baroque garden architecture in Slovenia.

The very respectable Gothic parish church is offset to the far north west of the outcrop. It was protected on one side by the adjacent castle building, on the other by the vicarage and sacristy tower, and all three defensive points were joined by the still extant wall.

New Radovljica expanded along the chestnut lined avenue which leads towards Lesce.

Latticework from nearby Kropa and statue of a boy from the main square in Radovljica

Kamnik (population 9,800)

Kamnik is an old town beneath the crown of the Kamnik Alps. It is first documented as a town in 1229, but a settlement undoubtedly existed earlier. Some of this distant past is revealed in the narrow streets of the old quarter, in the houses from hewn stone with portals and balconies, in the arcades and shop signs.

Supplementing this constructional romanticism, on a rocky hill in the centre of the town, is Mali grad (Little castle), with foundations going back to the 11th century. In the immediate vicinity of the ruins of the castle is a two storied chapel which is one of the most important and oldest Romanesque monuments in Slovenia. Adjacent to it is a crypt with frescoes from 1414. The Renaissance castle of Zaprice, which was rebuilt during the Baroque, contains

Kamnik, a good example of a well-preserved old market town, and its recreational hinterland of Velika planina

the permanent collection of Kamnik municipal museum. The town prides itself on having had its first school in far off 1391 and the first Slovene choir, Lira, in 1882, still in existence.

Curiously, Kamnik is more famous for its factories than its churches and castles, of which there are several in the vicinity.

Slovenj Gradec (population 6,800)

Slovenj Gradec is one of the oldest towns in Slovenia. It was probably a market before 1180 and was first mentioned as a town soon after. It developed in the middle of the basin bounded by the rivers Mislinja, Suhodolnica and Homš-nica. The town flourished culturally in the middle ages, numerous artisan craft masters worked in it and guilds of famous Carinthian carvers also operated in the town. A number of famous painters worked around here and left the town a rich heritage preserved in the churches and museums of Slovenj Gradec and

Slovenj Gradec lies in a wide basin with a very cold climate

its vicinity. The Gothic parish church from about the 15th century is a real gem. The composer Hugo Wolf was born in a house on the main square.

The cultural tradition of Slovenj Gradec is deliberately fostered with new initiatives. The gallery of art forged new cultural links in the sixties with an ambitious programme of international events and, by a document from the United Nations in 1989, the town was granted a place among towns with the title "Emissary of Peace".

Ptuj (population 11,300)

Ptuj has the status of a museum town. The oldest Slovene town, it obtained town rights in distant 977. Its monuments testify at every step to the far past, traces from Roman Poetovio and the periods which followed. The mighty 9th century castle above the river was once destroyed by the forerunners of the

The airfield in Slovenj Gradec is one of the most attractive sports airfields in Slovenia
A museum town. Ptuj, the oldest Slovene town

The Knight hall in Ptuj castle, with the best laid out museum in Slovenia

92 Hungarians, but is today well renovated. It houses a museum with major collections of musical instruments, tapestry, weapons and other historical treasures. One of the most beautiful monuments is in the town centre: Orpheus' monument, a Roman tombstone from the 2nd century AD. It was used as a penitents' stone and, since 1830, has been the centre of Ptuj's lapidary. Pride of place as the first open air museum belongs to the town tower, which became known as Povoden's museum, after Simon Povoden, on whose initiative Roman remains found in the vicinity were built into the foot of the tower.

There is no room to enumerate all Ptuj's monuments but two at least must be mentioned: the onetime Dominican monastery (today's Conservatory) in the west part of Ptuj, which contains a most beautiful eastern wing with vaulted cloisters, and the Minorite monastery in the east of the town. The former is one of the most beautiful early Gothic and early Baroque monuments in Slovenia, though unfortunately little of it remains, only the presbytery, which is renovated and still used for services.

Otočec on the Krka near Novo mesto; outside a castle, in side a hotel

Novo mesto (population 22,800)

The coat of arms of Novo mesto portrays Rudolf IV of Habsburg, who founded the town as Rudolphswerth in 1365. The name Novo mesto is from the 15th century. The town had an important defensive role during the Turkish incursions and it later became, and remained, the centre of Dolenjska.

The town was a favourite subject of the painter, Božidar Jakac, and it has been praised in words by such well known Slovenes as Janez Trdina, Dragotin Kette, Miran Jarc and Marijan Mušič. The funnel shaped square is particularly attractive, with arcaded passages both within and alongside the houses. The dominant Chapter Church, the oldest preserved building, is one of the great architectural monuments of Slovenia.

Novo mesto has two contrasting faces. One turned towards the Krka river and captured on canvas by Jakac, and the other whose features have been carved by Novo mesto industry. There has been considerable industrial

Novo mesto mirrored in the tranquil Krka river. A motif which excited an artist

development in recent decades, transforming the size of the town. Archeologists have excavated several important finds in the region of Novo mesto, including the bronze Hallstatt princely armour, more than 2,500 years old.

Metlika (population 3,300)

"Reggio que Metlica dicitur" dates back to 1228 and means "the region which is called Metlika". This is the origin of the name of the town not far from the river Kolpa and the Croatian border. In those days, the whole of Bela Krajina was called Metlika Marches, or Metlika in short. It experienced stormy times but, nevertheless, successfully developed into and remained a pleasant place, with all the charm of Bela krajina – the birches and vineyard slopes. There is still a strong tradition of folk habits and customs, and an abundance of historical monuments.

Metlika sits in a basin beside the border river of the Kolpa

The most picturesque view of Metlika old town opens up from the road along the former riverbed of the Bojica, from where one cane see a jumbled row of houses pressed hard against the old town wall. Part of the round defense tower is still preserved. To the south, the town facade is terminated by the "Komenda", a two-storey building of a former German Order of Chivalry. Attached to the Komenda is the Provost's House, a two-storey Baroque building from the first half of the 18th century. Nearby is the parish church where Frederik Baraga worked, the Metlika chaplain who later became famous as a missionary bishop among the American Indians.

The castle makes a powerful mark on Metlika. It now houses the Bela Krajina regional museum, the Slovene Firefighting Museum, and the Gangl exhibition. The skulptor, Alojz Gangl and the writer and teacher Engelbert Gangl were born in Gangl's house, where their memorial collection is housed.

Postojna (population 8200)

Postojna was made famous by Postojna cave, which began to attract tourists when it was officially opened in 1819. It has already been visited by 25 million people. The cave system to which it belongs measures 19.5 kilometres, and in extent is the ninth largest in Europe and the sixteenth in the world. It is named after the place where the cave starts, and this entrance part had already been visited by individuals in the middle ages, as witnessed by their signatures (the oldest is from 1213) in Imenski rov (Name gallery).

Postojna is first mentioned in old documents in 1226. In 1432, it is mentioned as a market, and it became a town in 1909. It is the centre of Karst tourism in Slovenia. The Institute for Karst research is here, which is housed in an old manor house in the middle of the main square, together with Notranjska museum, the history of which is equally closely connected with Postojna cave. The parish church of St. Štefan is not far from here.

Around 25 million people have visited Postojna cave over a period of almost 180 years

Postojna – a town on an important traffic route through the Postojna gate

Postojna had an exceptionally important traffic role for centuries, since the trade route from Ljubljana towards the littoral and Italian cities led through the so-called Postojna gate. When the Ljubljana–Razdrto motorway was opened, traffic through Postojna appreciably diminished. However, there has been no decrease in visits to Postojna cave, whose stalactite system of several hundred thousand years old is one of the most magnificent in the world. There are also occasional concerts held here, including a pre-Christmas nativity concert.

Nova Gorica (population 14700)

The dividing line between Slovenia and Italy, drawn on the basis of the Paris Peace Treaty of 1947, was "godfather" to the birth of Nova Gorica. That split into two what had been until then the fairly unified economic space of Gorizia. Slovenia lost Gorizia, but soon decided to build a new town in the area of Divje poljane (Wild fields), which were overgrown with high swamp grasses and which had in places to be drained. They started to build the first housing blocks in 1948.

Bourbon kings rest in Kostanjevica monastery by Nova Gorica

Nova Gorica, the new town on the Slovene side of the border with Italy

Nova Gorica first officially received its name as a settlement in 1949. It quickly grew and became the centre of a large part of the Soča region and an important road and rail crossroads at the meeting point of the Soča and Vipava valleys.

Nova Gorica has been called the town of flowers, and the arts have also "blossomed" there. A new theatre was opened in 1994, and the town obtains a special image from its cultural monuments; especially numerous along the "alley of famous Primorska men". A monument to the first Slovene airman and aircraft constructor, Edvard Rusjan, who made his first flight in 1909 on Veliki Roje by Gorica, stands in the central town park, not far from the municipal assembly, which is embellished with statues by Boris Kalin.

To the south, the town looks onto Kostanjevica, where there is a large Franciscan monastery in which a Bourbon king is buried; to the east it is closed by the Kromberk hills (the Gorica museum is in Kromberk); to the north is Sv. Katarina hill with a viewing platform an restaurant Kekec; and to the west Nova Gorica borders on Gorizia. Despite the state border, the two towns are closely connected, with many links of friendship and joint presentations. Since the largest casino in Slovenia was opened in Nova Gorica – Perla – the town has become a gambling mecca, especially for the neighbouring Italians.

Tolmin (population 3800)

Tolmin only became a market in 1820, and a town in 1952. Its history is closely intertwined with the history of the Tolmin region, which is apparent from its unconventional Slovene character, since this small area has always been something special. A small settlement in the middle of the Tolmin basin is evidenced as early as 1065. Tolmin itself nestles on the highest terrace at the confluence of the Soča and the Tolminka. Because of the roads which connect

Tolmin – a town in the middle of the mountains, the centre of the Upper Soča region

The Pust carnival has a special place in Tolmin. — Detail from the painted facade of Coronini castle

it to Zgornje Posočje (Upper Soča region), it was an administrative centre, and at the same time a craft-trade centre, which has been economically strengthened in recent decades and has become simultaneously the cultural centre of the Upper Soča region.

Tolmin is also of tourist interest, since here is the start of the marked trail into the Krn mountains and to the peaks of the Lower Bohinj mountains. Nearby are Tolminska Korita (Tolmin channels) with the only hot spring in Primorska, and sixty metres above the Tolminka, Hudičev most (Devil's bridge) leads over gorge. A rise called Kozlov rob (Goat's brink), immediately beside the town, offers a fine view, and a prehistoric fortress and the ruins of the main castle in Tolmin, which had already fallen into disrepair in the 16th century when its owners built a new castle in the middle of the settlement, were discovered here. The Tolmin museum collection, under the auspices of the Gorica museum, is on view in this latter, Coronini's castle. Mementoes of Dante are also preserved in the museum. The nearby Dante's cave is named after him, since there is a legend that it was right here that Dante obtained the inspiration for his description of Hell in his Divine Comedy.

A narrow trail leads from Tolmin to Javorca, where there is one of the most beautiful chapels from the time of the first world war. The biggest mountain battle in history took place along the Soča, and the well-ordered cemetery in Tolmin is a reminder of those who fell on the Soča front.

Velenje (population 27300)

Velenje is a model of a modern industrial town with two quite different faces. One is of more recent date and has a modern urban plan and modern architecture. New Velenje was founded after 1954, when urban planners planned a new settlement in the south-eastern part of the Šalek valley, on a green plain, in the conviction that increased mining of coal would require housing for 20,000 new inhabitants. In 1975, total production already exceeded four million tons, and then climbed to more than five million tons. Velenje miners became and have remained the largest group of miners in Slovenia. So it is hardly surprising that some say that coal made this town!

Rich lignite mines and a strong electro-technical industry have set Velenje among the larger Slovene towns. It also has its own history (below)

That the Šalek valley is rich in coal was first reported by Father Steiz in the second half of the 18th century.

The other face is provided by the old town core, which hugs the flanks of the 66 metre high hill on which the castle stands. This was first mentioned in 1275, but the settlement below it even earlier. Velenje castle now contains a museum with permanent collections, one of which presents the development of Slovene mining from the middle of the 18th century to today. A reconstruction of a prehistoric mammoth, one the most important of such finds in Europe, is one of its attractions. The remains were found in 1964, near Velenje.

Brežice (population 6900)

There are more than a hundred castles in Slovenia, and one of the best preserved and arranged is in Brežice. It contains the largest secular Baroque painted space in Slovenia – the knights hall, 35 metres long and 10 metres

Brežice, the last Slovene town on the Sava, does not hide its Pannonian origins

wide. The original medieval castle was burned by rebellious peasants in the 16th century, but a new one was built in its place. It is a fine example of fortified Renaissance castle architecture, with mighty circular defence towers at the corners. It contains the Posavje museum, which presents the history of places along the Sava, especially the history of the peasant revolts, and it also has rich archeological and ethological collections, as well as a collection of Baroque art and a memorial exhibition to the painter, Franjo Stiplovšek. Cultural performances are also held in the castle.

The settlement grew up beside the castle, and was given the name "civitas Rein", meaning town on the banks of the river. The Slovene name, Brežice has the same derivation. The river meant that there was lively traffic in the town, since there was formerly a landing place in Brežice. Trade also had an important role. Two storey houses predominate along the main street, and low

Brežice castle, in which some valuable art treasures are concealed

102 single storey houses, which are today a reminder of the former appearance of the town, grew up on the ruins of the eastern town wall. Brežice is mentioned as a town from 1322, and it was supposed to have been founded after 1200 on the long promontory above the former channel of the Sava.

The water tower is a protected monument. Together with the castle it is identified by the name, Brežice. The funnel-shaped square is an urban planning particularity of the town. The longest bridge across the Sava in Slovenia is close to the town, and the lively spa, Čateške toplice, is also not far away.

Murska Sobota (population 13900)

Murska Sobota is the most northerly town of Slovenia; at the same time, it is the centre of Pomurje, which embraces the region along the Mura between the Austrian and Hungarian borders. It became a town (civitas) in 1366, but long had the appearance of a Pannonian village settlement. It began to get its contemporary appearance in the last century, though it has had the pulse of a real town only in the last fifty years, due in part to the industrial giants, Mura and ABC Pomurka. There are almost no traces left of the former extended

A fair number of members of the Evangelical church live in Prekmurje. They have a fine church in Murska Sobota

The central square in Murska Sobota shows that the town has not experienced pressure for space

village. This was named after land which was called Belmura (Inner Mura) in the middle of the 13th century. The name Sobota appeared in 1297. The town has "sprung up" between the parish church and the castle.

Belmura manor is supposed to have already been standing in 1255, and a castle was later built on the same site. It is first mentioned in 1498, was given its present groundplan only in the 16th century, and was completed in the first half of the 18th century. It is surrounded by an extensive park. It belonged to the powerful Szapary family for more than 300 years, and the last owner, Count Laszlo, sold it to the Sobota municipality, who devoted it to the museum.

The collected museum material presents the unique historical path which Pomurje experienced and which marked this tiny corner of Slovene lands with originality and uniqueness, also because of the visible Hungarian influence and from being cut off from Slovenia (by the Mura!). Numerous other monuments in Murska Sobota also testify to this.

⊖ border crossing	☒ health spa
⊕ airport	✳ ski resort
✝ sports airfield	◮ camp

Land of Green Tourism

Whatever peace is promised visitors by Slovenia, with its unspoilt nature, nature reserves, the home comforts of farm tourism, in pubs with good food and intentionally modest sized hotels, visiting it could also be an interesting mixture of recreation and exciting excursions. The land itself encourages it; the close proximity of different regions, so that it really is feasible after breakfast beneath the crowns of Alpine firs, to lunch for a change under the Mediterranean sun, or after lunch among the vineyard slopes on the edge of the Pannonian plain, to zip to the Karst for supper, where the wines are different. It's all very close, even Venice and Vienna or Salzburg, the three most common day trips to bring a breath of culture to lazy holidays. Pleasure in close contact with nature and the vicinity of completely different worlds – this is what Slovenia has to offer the tourist.

The Špik group above Martuljek – one of the most beautiful mountain groups in the Alps – is among the most unspoilt parts of Triglav National Park

Rogaška Slatina, a health spa with tradition

Radenci (upper) and Moravci (lower), attractive tourist centres on the Pannonian plains

With nature to health

Spas are the cradle of tourism; established in the last century, the whole culture of holiday making is here different from the coastal resorts and sports centres which emerged after the second world war. Something remained behind the factory masters and aristocracy, the initiators of the cult of health from nature: a call to sublime peace and a dignified pace which is not distracted by instant pleasure. Slovenia has several spas dating from this time: Rogaška Slatina, Radenci and Dolenjske Toplice – old spa complexes which were later joined by Čateške Toplice, Podčetrtek and Moravci. Even Bled, today more of a popular tourist resort, was at first a spa and heart patients still go to Portorož by the sea. The peace and decorum are here just as they were a hundred years ago. What is different is the new saunas, pools, tennis courts and gymnasiums, and the increasingly sophisticated medical facilities that ensure that guests, patients, receive the most up-to-date treatment available.

A century and a half after the Swiss, Arnold Rikli, brought the first international guest to a health spa, Bled is still worth a visit

The pleasure of movement

Countless mountain trails and forest tracks provide an unlimited source of more or less demanding mountain trips. Those in the Julian, Kamnik and Savinja Alps are the most spectacular, but trips through the foothills are also very pleasant, especially along the European E6 and E7 Footpaths. River rapids are a bold challenge for kayak and canoe enthusiasts, since routes of differing grades of difficulty provide opportunities for both beginners and experienced sportsmen. The finest runs are on the river Soča and its gorges.

The ski resorts of Bled, Bovec, Bohinj, Kranjska Gora, Krvavec, Rogla and Pohorje come alive in winter. Slovenia has a long skiing tradition and the world skiing elite gather every year in Kranjska Gora and Maribor for World Cup races in the Alpine disciplines, and for skijumping in Planica. Slovenia is an experienced organiser of European and world sports competitions.

Favourable air currents offer unique potential for hang- and paragliding, and ballooning is a sport which has begun to take hold in Slovenia. Mountain tourist centres have recently started holding courses for beginners in hang- and paragliding, as well as providing guided climbing tours. The north wall of Triglav, the highest face in the Julian Alps, is a popular challenge for climbers. Bled and Lipica, Mokrice and Rogaška Slatina have exclusive golf courses.

Slovenia is a real paradise for hunting and fishing enthusiasts. Lynx, red deer and bear are the main game in Kočevje forest, chamois and ibex in the Alps, while the lowlands of Prekmurje offer abundant pheasant, roe deer and boar. Lynx, reintroduced to Slovenia some decades ago and still protected, have become quite widespread. For fishermen, there are plenty of almost perfect lakes, streams and rivers full of fish, but Soča trout and grayling are considered to be in a class of their own, as sport and supper alike.

The long winters and fine terrain close to the Slovene-Austrian-Italian triple border have given rise to major ski resorts

Kranjska Gora is also a starting point for mountain tours

Farm tourism – an attractive form of holiday

Recreation in unspoilt nature, hunting and fishing, offer plenty of pleasure to enthusiasts
Golf at Bled. Slovenia has three other courses

Bernardin tourist settlement by Portorož
Sailing competition along Slovene coast

The sea and Karst

The tourist centre of the Slovene coast is the summer and spa resort of Portorož, with a marina and nearby Istrian and Italian marinas from Pula and Trieste to Venice. Its hinterland has been placed on the UNESCO list of the world's natural heritage. The Karst, the rocky landscape after which karst phenomena throughout the world have been named, is most breathtaking in the caves of Vilenica, Škocjan and Postojna. The latter two are particularly attractive. Škocjan is precipitous cliffs and gorges where, far below the paths cut into the face, the underground river winds several kilometres through a string of underground passages and caverns. Postojna cave fascinates with gigantic white stalactites and stalagmites. There is more in chapter one about the polje by Cerknica, which is half a year a lake and the other half a plain. Lipica, on the Karst, is the home of the famous Lipizzaners, the ceremonial horses of the Vienna court. The large studfarm near the village of Lipica has a covered parade ring, open air rings and extensive excellent terrain in the vicinity.

Marina at Portorož, a perfect starting point for yachting on the Adriatic

Postojna cave with white stalactites and stalagmites is a world famous wonder
Lipica. From where the white Vienna court horses came

Masters
of Individual Sports

Ski competitions start with winter; one of most popular sports in Slovenia

It would be an exaggeration to claim that the Slovenes can be so closely linked to sport as the Finns, but sport, not least because of the bond it creates with nature, is certainly very dear to the Slovene heart. Sport developed in Slovenia with the time lag that has applied in most fields, with its own characteristics giving it local and national colour.

Writ among the stars

In 1689, J. V. Valvasor wrote in "In Praise of the Duchy of Carniola" that in his time, there were shooting competitions, and his note on Bloke skiing is particularly detailed and enthusiastic. Excluding the northern peoples, especially the Laps and Norwegians, the people of the Bloke plateau and hills were the first in Europe to use skis, both as a means of transport and for recreation.

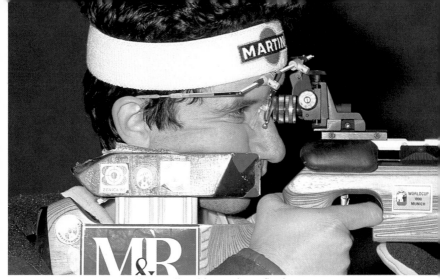

Rajmond Debevec, holder of several world records in rifle shooting

True competitive sport only started in Slovenia in the twentieth century. The first Slovene to win a medal in Slovene colours was a gymnast, Karel Fuchs, in 1909 in Luxembourg, and the first Olympic medal was won by a fencer, Rudolf Cvetko, who received a silver medal in the Olympic Games in Stockholm in 1912 as part of the Austrian sabre team. The flag of the Yugoslav state was first hoisted and the anthem played, in honour of the Slovene gymnast, Leon Štukelj, in Paris in 1924, where he became Olympic inter-disciplinary champion. He also won a gold medal at these Olympics on the horizontal bar.

Sports activities after the second world war achieved new popularity and heights. Organisation improved with the creation of the Sports Association of Slovenia, with about 3,000 member clubs and societies, and Slovenia already had a faculty for sports teachers and professionals. Well-established disciplines produced new champions: gymnast Miro Cerar collected 30 honours at major competitions, including two Olympic gold medals. In the sixties, Ivo Daneu became a world basketball star. Athlete Draga Stamejčič set a world 80 metres hurdles record, and the swimming brothers, Borut and Darjan Petrič,

Basketball. The only ballgame which has brought a world champion's title to Ljubljana. – Slovenia has many top classical and free climbers

Mountaineering is the most popular activity. From spring to late autumn

Rowing, a sport in which the Slovenes have been winners. At the Olympic games in Barcelona, 1992, Iztok Čop and Denis Žvegelj won bronze medals

won medals in the crawl at European and world competitions. Marksman Rajmond Debevec is a world record holder and winner of many world cup shooting competitions. Oarsmen, Miro Steržaj, Boris Urbanc and Marika Kardinar, have collected gold medals at world championships, and Slovene boats won bronze medals in both the coxless fours and coxless pairs at the Barcelona Olympics, the first at which Slovenia appeared as a sovereign state. With the exception of the basketball player, Daneu, they are all masters of individual sports disciplines, like whitewater kajak, rowing, parachuting, and the combat sports, in which Slovenes have often been among the world's champions.

Mountaineering, a great love of the Slovenes – the mountaineering association of Slovenia, with 100,000 members, is the most popular sports organisation – is at the very peak of Alpine climbing. Top Slovene climbers have achieved sensational ascents of the world's highest mountains and most

The Slovenia Open tournament in Domžale. The first major tennis event in our parts

demanding faces. The best of them, Tomo Česen, is currently considered the leading world alpinist.

Kingdom of skis

On 24 February 1961, on the highest ski jump in the world in Obersdorf, Jože Šlibar, a 27 year old student of forestry, jumped 141 metres and set a new world record. This was the first time that an achievement of a Slovene skier was world news. The reputation of Planica – the cradle of skijumping – was validated. It was necessary to wait another twenty years for the next really great successes in skiing when, in Schladming in 1982, at the world cup competition in Alpine skiing, the first two skiers from Slovenia stood on the winning podium: the ice was broken by Boris Strel, third in giant slalom, and Bojan Križaj won the silver in slalom, being second to the legendary Swedish skier, Ingemar Stenmark, who remained faithful to the Slovene firm of Elan throughout his matchless career as a top competitor.

The first Olympic medal followed in Sarajevo in 1984. Jure Franko skied to second place in the giant slalom and, four years later, in 1988 in Calgary, the Slovene ski jumpers effectively made their mark. Matjaž Debelak won the bronze on the big jump, the Yugoslav team (only Slovenes) leaped to a silver medal in the team competition, behind the unbeatable Finnish team. This was also the period when the ladies' ski team established themselves, since Mateja Svet gave Slovene skiing a star the like of which there have been few in skiing history. After several awards in Crans Montana in 1987 and the Olympic silver in Canada in 1988, the 20 year old Ljubljana girl became world slalom champion in 1989 in Vail. Her achievement was repeated by the exceptionally talented, not yet 20 ski-jumper, Franci Petek, at the next world championship in Val di Fiemme in 1991.

Planica. Cradle of ski jumping and the first to carry man beyond the magic 100 meters, recently also over 200 meters

The Slovene skiers Alenka Dovžan, Katja Koren (above) and Jure Košir (below) earned three bronze medals at the winter Olympic Games at Lillehammer in 1994

There are currently around 300,000 skiing enthusiasts in Slovenia, quite a high proportion of a population of only 2 million. It is no more a national sport but an identity: every year, each Slovene buys at least one ticket for the Skiing Lottery, and so supports the national team which first competed under the flag of the new state at the XVIth Olympic Games in Albertville and finally earned three bronze medals at Lillehammer in 1994.

ROGER METCALFE

An Englishman in Slovenia

The author, an Englishman, has lived in Ljubljana since 1991

Life to Slovene taste and measure: houses with well laid out gardens in the small town of Grosuplje

The youngest country in the world, a title of curious merit attached to Slovenia after its achievement of independence in 1991, is, ironically, peopled by one of the oldest and most diverse nations in Europe. It is a modern, progressive democracy, with every likelihood of joining the mainstream of European integration, but at the same time it retains the unique features of a tiny nation that has not only survived a millenium of foreign influence and domination, but has in fact emerged as a potential winner in the new order that arrived at the start of the nineties.

To many, Slovenia is simply a political statement. The country which fought off Serbian-dominated socialist hegemony, the shining example of an "East" European nation with a relatively efficient economy which stood up and said no to communism. But this is, although an essential part of the nation's history, an increasing irrelevance.

Slovenia was never a truly communist state, just as it was never a truly Hapsburg dominion. The complexity of Slovene politics, and the range of democratic debate raging in the country's Assembly every day, point not to an emerging democracy, as we would patronizingly conclude, but to a nation which has always preserved a sophistication and appreciation of the highest principles of a modern, civilised society.

From its Alpine peaks to its Adriatic coast, its Pannonian plains to the undulating lowlands, Slovenia has the capacity to draw in the outsider, to charm, amaze, infuriate and, in short, to do all those things which one would only normally associate with the greater nations of the old world. The difference here is firstly the polite and usually bright way the Slovenes deal with outsiders, and secondly the essential distance they maintain, as part of an ancient ritual of self-preservation.

Slovenia is a young country

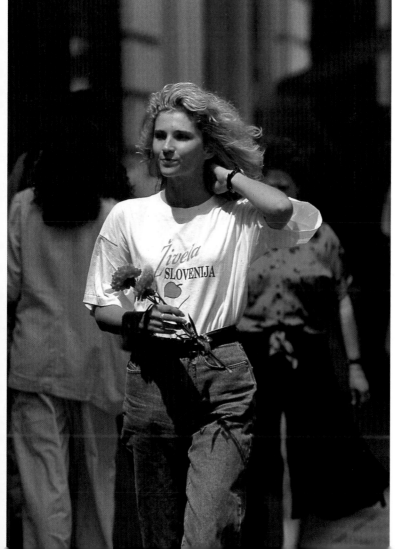

Triglav National Park, an Alpine nature reserve, is an attempt to preserve unspoilt, 85,000 hectares of mountain landscape

The capital

Slovenia is not heavily urbanised, but its cities and towns are old and full of character. Of all Slovenia's cities, it is Ljubljana which dominates and sets the pace for the lifestyle of the urban Slovene. Ljubljana is also the first place people usually come to in Slovenia, and is also probably the best-known city in this part of Europe.

The splendour of Ljubljana's theatres, squares and parks is matched, as a rule, by the chic intelligence of its people. Of course you see all types, old people, young people, drunks, punks, thrusting managers and supercilious secretaries, but the pervading image is of a vibrant city, home to myriad cultures and art forms, hugging the banks of the dreamy, willow-lined Ljubljanica river. People from all over Slovenia come here to study, to soak up the beauty of what earlier architects started to call the Slovene Athens, and to get in on the act of Ljubljana's transformation into one of the most forward-looking and dynamic cities in central Europe.

It is dangerous to think that Ljubljana is a microcosm of Slovenia, for it is something of a hybrid as capital cities go. The decaying (and decadent) Baroque grandeur conspires with the almost futuristic motifs – curious pyramids, fantastical classical monoliths – to make the most hard-headed visitor stand back and puzzle over its source.

Of course, if you trap a Ljubljana native – and their usual intelligent geniality on the street makes this a simple task – your interlocutor will smile in that wise Slovene way and pronounce "Plečnik". "What-nik?" comes your reply. "Jože Plečnik, our famous architect, the great exponent of the Viennese Secession." Up until his death in 1957, and mainly in the period between the two world wars, he transformed Ljubljana's visage into the extraordinary agglomeration of Classical fragments which so startle the visitor. The Tromos-

Gaudeamus. Around 90,000 matriculants annually

tovje (Three Bridges) complex is one of Plečnik's most notable – and uncontroversially attractive – legacies in the splendid heart of the city, while the National and University Library (NUK) on Vega street just to the south is a remarkable, but not quite so popular creation in red brick and Doric.

Whatever Plečnik's singular masonic fantasies may have done to Ljubljana, we can forgive him when we come to the socialist realist monolith called Republic Square (quietly but quickly renamed from Revolution Square). As its former name suggests, visitors will feel as though they are suddenly being projected back twenty years, and only the exquisitely dressed shoppers and ministerial yuppies traversing the carpark and pavements will remind you of Slovenia's quirky free-market dynamism.

Ljubljana does not look like a city going through convulsive changes, but in many ways it is. Shiny plaques tacked onto crumbling facades speak of the new entrepreneurial spirit – or rather of the newly respectable pursuit of profit

Every spring there is an exhibition of old cameras in Ljubljana's Križanke

– and of new ministries, still in their first flush of (relatively) uncorrupted idealism. Then, of course, there are the street names. New maps are available, but if you have an appointment in the centre of town do not be surprised if you are given three different addresses for the same place.

Other things appear to be in a state of transformation in Ljubljana, most notably its castle perched on the hill that pops up out of the old town like some ancient toy. The cranes, the scaffolding and the acres of concrete and mud belie the fact that the renovation has already been going on for many years. Inside Ljubljana castle, visitors can sip tea or gossip over an aperitif in the renovated, brutalist iron and stone cafe. Outside, the tower offers possibly one of the most magnificent views in Europe, not only of the exquisitely compact city but across a broad sweep of central Slovenia right up to the mighty Alpine border with Austria.

The path which encircles Ljubljana, among the green suburbs of the city, is a popular recreation area

The war of independence

Ljubljana castle is an excellent place from which to reflect for a moment on the war – for Slovenes it is just THE WAR – of June/July 1991 and on the whole trauma of Yugoslavia. For Slovenes it is a sad and hurtful issue, particularly since they maintain with justification that their conduct throughout the affair was honourable and reasonable. It is much simpler for the foreigner: mere incomprehension.

If you look across this delicate city from the castle, it is impossible to encompass the thought of the death and destruction which so nearly engulfed the nation in June 1991. Every Slovene has his or her war story, but it must be stressed that these people do not dwell on the subject. During the conflict, the obvious fatuousness of the federal Yugoslav machinations and the bungling and brutish military adventure by the federal army saved the Slovenes the

Fire from the castle above Ljubljana

necessity of arguing their case. Indeed, their task became essentially one of preserving the psychological advantage which the Slovene nation had clearly enjoyed for some time before the use of arms.

This inevitable reflection on the convulsions of 1991 marks an appropriate point for a brief excursion into the Slovene mentality, which came to the fore at no time more than during its battle for independence. The ordinary Slovene may on an ordinary day appear to be rather a fussy type, verging perhaps on the parochial and apparently rather unadventurous. Beware the external appearance, however. When their war with the federals started, out of the very woodwork, it seemed, came a nation that was suddenly galvanised, cool, efficient and deadly successful. The rabbits of the northern republic, as they were called by the Yugoslav army, stood up to be counted, nobody complained, nobody showed fear, nobody was intimidated.

Overnight, barricades appeared, and the fine tuning of the local Territorial Defence Force was evident; not at all in their equipment and resources, which were pitiful by anyone's standards, but in the clear discipline, the quiet professionalism on the faces of the territorials, as well as the way in which people from all walks of life had come together to defend something which, to the obvious surprise of the aggressor, was serious and precious. It took only ten days for the Slovene to make their point.

The pace of daily life

Slovenia is very traditional and life is lived in the family circle. Unlike northern Europeans or Americans, the Slovenes stay very closely bonded to their families, and in many ways the family ties, particularly parents and children and brothers and sisters, remain the most powerful emotional anchors throughout the life of the average Slovene.

The positive aspect of this is, of course, the sense of support and stability which the strong family bond gives these people. On the negative side, there is a tendency for Slovenes to develop certain forms of emotional independence rather later and less securely than in other cultures. Many foreigners who stay for a longer time in Slovenia are surprised at the power parents hold over their children, and at the same time, they are possibly envious of all the props and benefits young Slovenes can expect from their elders.

Many countries could claim to be racial melting pots, but few with as much proof in such a concentrated area as Slovenia. This little piece of south-central Europe, wedged between the Alps and the Adriatic, features wiry mountain types, stocky Magyars, swarthy Italians, tall, fair northerners and broad-faced easterners, all with a hint of that philosophical Slav demeanour.

The cities, of course, present the greatest concentrations of this Slovene diversity, and they are supplemented by the immigrant communities primarily from the other former Yugoslav republics. In the apartment blocks of Maribor, Celje and Ljubljana, you can hear Albanian, Serbo-Croat (nowadays referred to only as Serb or Croatian), Macedonian, Italian and Hungarian, as well as the startling range of different Slovene dialects.

Down in the markets, guttural south Slav voices mingle with the rich lilt of

Market by Ljubljana cathedral

"Ohcet" (marriage) in Ljubljana. Old customs can be adapted, but never forgotten

It happens several times a year: a meeting of hundreds of mountain lovers

northern, Germanic accents and the constant importuning babble of the Croatian vegetable sellers. Large, blonde matrons giggle and tease small, sinewy mountain men, and the ubiquitous moustachioed, green-uniformed watchmen add their own imperial dignity to the hubbub.

Back in the streets, the bigger cities vibrate with the self-conscious beauty of Slovenia's younger generations, immaculately bedecked in thigh-Length suede boots and designer jackets. You will see black hair, blonde hair and red hair, but above all, well-groomed hair. Sharp, space age glasses perched on aquiline noses suggest a hard, go-getting nature which does not in fact do justice to the Slovene capacity for modesty and politeness.

Alongside the Anglo-Saxon graffiti, Ljubljana — and other cities — boasts a wealth of spray-painted poetry of a suprisingly high standard which, sadly, the arbiters of civic taste saw fit to remove just before the grand independence celebrations of June 1991. The curious thing is that Slovenes both young and old stop to read these playful messages; whereas an advertising hoarding erected nearby in the centre of Ljubljana, and featuring an artist's lurid impression of a bimbo leaning over a fast car, mysteriously ended up in the

A witness of the times. Quiet refuges in the middle of nature

Ljubljanica river one night. The Slovenes give the clear impression that they know what is right for them.

Slovenia is one of the best examples on our planet of a world in miniature. Apart from its geography, which prompts locals to boast of skiing in the morning and scuba diving in the afternoon, its complexity of language and culture is so concentrated as to defy comparison. Travel fifty kilometres in any direction in Slovenia and you will enter a different dialect zone, complete with different customs, industries and architecture. The impression confirms the historical background to Slovenia – a small nation struggling for survival while giants all around rampaged through the country, stamping their own culture here and fighting over this small parcel of Europe like children with a rag doll. In earlier times, this impression spoke of the vulnerability and fragility of the Slovenes, but nowadays it points simply to the richness and range of the country's resources and culture.

Land on the sunny side of the Alps – this time in snow

Basic data on Slovenia

Area: 20,256 km^2
Population (31.12.1993): 1,989,400
Number of households (1991): 640,200
Population density: 98 inhab./km^2
Constitutional order: parliamentary republic
Capital: Ljubljana
Ethnic composition: (census 1991) Slovene 87.8%, Hungarian 0.43%, Italian 0.16%
Official language: Slovene, in nationally mixed regions also Hungarian and Italian
Currency: Slovene tolar (1 SIT = 100 stotin)
Annual population growth (1993): – 0.1 per thousand
Birthrate (1993): 9.9 per thousand

Life expectancy (1992–93): 69.4 years for men, 77.29 years for women
Urban population (1991): 50.5%
Major towns (1993): Ljubljana (276,200), Maribor (108,100), Celje (41,300), Kranj (37,300), Velenje (27,100), Koper (25,300), Novo mesto (22,800)
Gross domestic product (1993): 12.67 billion USD
Gross domestic product per inhabitant (1993): 6,366 USD
Main farm products (1993): potatoes (367,000t), corn (249,000t), wheat (168,000t), hops (3,400t), apples (91,000t), grapes (128,000t), wine (635,000hl), meat (139,000t), milk (5.33 mill hl)
Main industrial sectors (by share of added value in industry, 1992): food industry 14.6%, textiles 12.1%, metal working 11.3%, electrotechnical and electronics 10.9%, chemical industry 9.0%, machine industry 7.5%, paper and graphics industry 7.4%
Exports (1994): 6750 million USD
Imports (1994): 7200 million USD
Number of tourists (1993): 1,450,000, number of overnight stays: 5,385,000
Number of schools (1992/1993): primary 822, middle 145, universities 2
Number of pupils/students (1992/93): primary school 217,400, middle school 95,600, colleges 3,800, universities 24,300
Number of books published (1993): 2440
Number of newspapers (1992): 641, of which five dailies and 31 weeklies.
Number of television subscribers (1993): 454,000
Number of telephone subscribers (1993): 528,000
Number of motor vehicles registered (1993): 793,000, of which 633,000 private cars

Useful Information

CLIMATE: Alpine, Continental, Mediterranean
January average temperature
mountain region   below 0 °C
interior   from 0 to 2 °C
coast   from 2 to 4 °C
July average temperature
interior   from 20 to 22 °C
coast   from 22 to 24 °C
Average annual rainfall
from 800 mm in the east to 3000 mm in the northwest

AVERAGE ALTITUDE: 600 m
The highest mountain: Triglav 2864 m

NATIONAL HOLIDAYS IN SLOVENIA
January 1 & 2   New Year
February 8   Prešeren Day, Slovene day of culture
April 27   Resistance Day
May 1 & 2   Bank holiday
June 25   National Day
November 1   Day of remembrance of the dead
December 26   Independence Day

OTHER HOLIDAYS
Easter   (Sunday and Monday)
Whitsunday   (Sunday)
August 15   Feast of the Assumption
October 31   Reformation Day
December 25   Christmas

LANGUAGE
The official language is Slovene and in nationally mixed regions also Hungarian and Italian. In contacts with foreigners, Slovenes use English, German, Italian and French.

CURRENCY
The currency is the Slovene tolar (SIT). 1 SIT = 100 stotin. Foreign currency may be exchanged at border crossings, in banks, exchanges and hotels.

ENTRY
There are 64 international border crossings which are open non-stop. Foreigners travelling with a valid passport may stay in Slovenia for three months or until the expiry of the visa. Travellers from the EC and Austria may also enter with an identity card.

WORKING HOURS
Shops are open from 08.00 to 20.00, on Saturdays to 13.00. Some private shops are also open in the mornings on Sundays and holidays. Banks are open from 8.00 to 12.00 and from 14.00 to 17.00, on Saturday to 12.00.

Useful Addresses

**CHAMBER OF ECONOMY
OF SLOVENIA**
Slovenska 41, 61000 Ljubljana
tel. (+386) 61 1250 122
fax (+386) 61 218 242

**BANKA SLOVENIJE (BANK
OF SLOVENIA)**
Slovenska 35, 61000 Ljubljana
tel. (+386) 61 215 448
fax (+386) 61 215 516

WORLD TRADE CENTER
Dunajska 156, 61000 Ljubljana
tel. (+386) 61 344 666
fax (+386) 61 16 83 480

SLOVENE EXPORT ASSOCIATION
Josipine Turnograjske 6,
61000 Ljubljana
tel. (+386) 61 17 62 019
fax (+386) 61 12 53 015

**CENTER FOR INTERNATIONAL
COOPERATION AND
DEVELOPMENT**
Kardeljeva ploščad 1,
61000 Ljubljana
tel. (+386) 61 16 83 597
fax (+386) 61 343 696

**AVTO MOTO ZVEZA SLOVENIJE
(AUTOMOBILE ASSOCIATION
– Information)**
Dunajska 128, 61000 Ljubljana
tel. (+386) 61 341 341
fax (+386) 61 342 378
Help, information, touring service: 987

RADIO SLOVENIJA
Tavčarjeva 17, 61000 Ljubljana
tel. (+386) 61 13 11 333
fax (+386) 61 13 34 007
Program 1: 88,5, 90,0, 91,8, 92,9,
94,1 MHz
Program 2: 92,4, 93,5,96,9, 97,6, 98,9,
99,9 MHz
Program 3: 96,5, 101,4, 102,0 MHz

LJUBLJANA BRNIK AIRPORT
64210 Brnik, Slovenija
tel. (+386) 64 222 700
fax (+386) 64 221 220

RAILWAY STATION LJUBLJANA
Trg OF, 61000 Ljubljana
tel. (+386) 61 316 768
fax (+386) 61 319 141

BUS STATION LJUBLJANA
Trg OF 4, 61000 Ljubljana
tel. (+386) 61 13 36 136

**KOMPAS INTERNATIONAL,
Tourist Agency**
Pražakova 4, 61000 Ljubljana
tel. (+386) 61 13 27 127
fax (+386) 61 320 669

KOMPAS-HERZ RENT-A-CAR
Celovška 206, 61000 Ljubljana
tel. (+386) 61 15 91 311
fax (+386) 61 15 92 442

**TOURIST INFORMATION CENTER
LJUBLJANA (TIC)**
Slovenska 35, 61000 Ljubljana
tel. (+386) 61 215 412
fax (+386) 61 222 115

**TOURIST INFORMATION CENTER
MARIBOR (MATIC)**
Grajski trg 1, 62000 Maribor
Telefon (+386) 62 21 262
Telefax (+386) 62 25 271

Diplomatic Offices in Slovenia

March 1995

ALBANIA
Ljubljana, Ob Ljubljanici 12
tel. 061/132 23 24, 132 20 53
fax 061/132 31 29

AUSTRIA
Ljubljana, Štrekljeva 5
tel. 061/213 436, 213 412
fax 061/221 717

BELGIUM
Ljubljana, Snežniška 10
tel. 061/219 210
fax 061/219 210

BOSNIA & HERZEGOVINA
Ljubljana, Likozarjeva 6
tel. 061/150 122 (GZS)
fax 061/13 22 230

BULGARIA
Ljubljana, Jesenkova 2
tel. 061/133 11 49, 133 12 09
fax 061/133 72 61

CENTRAL AFRICAN REPUBLIC
Ljubljana, V Murglah 15
tel. 061/331 538

CHILE
Ljubljana, Brdnikova 34b
tel. 061/271 159
fax 061/263 280

CHINA
61103 Ljubljana,
Stara Slovenska ulica 1
tel. 061/140 23 83
fax 061/140 40 07

CROATIA
Gruberjevo nabrežje 6
tel. 061/125 72 87, 125 62 20
fax 061/125 81 06

CZECH REPUBLIC
Ljubljana, Avčinova 4
tel. in fax 061/132 80 35, 318 423

DENMARK
Ljubljana, Resljeva 24/I
tel. 061/311 236, 313 740
fax 13 37 098

**EUROPEAN UNION, Delegation
of the European Commission**
Ljubljana, Trg republike 3/XI
tel. 061/125 13 03
fax 061/125 20 85

FINLAND
61230 Domžale, Bevkova 11
tel. in fax 061/713 297

FRANCE
Ljubljana, Železna c. 18/VI
tel. 061/173 44 41, 173 44 31
fax 061/173 44 42

GERMANY
Ljubljana, Prešernova 27
tel. 061/216 166 (Embassy)
061/222 093 (Visa Department)
fax 061/125 42 10

GREAT BRITAIN
Ljubljana, Trg republike 3/IV
tel. 061/125 71 91, 125 31 66
fax 061/125 01 74

GREECE
Ljubljana, Dalmatinova 2/XIV
tel. 061/302 591, 314 376
fax 061/313 182

HUNGARY
Ljubljana, Dunajska 22/IV
tel. 061/131 51 68, 131 60 63
fax 061/131 71 43

ITALY
Ljubljana, Snežniška 8
tel. 061/126 21 94, 126 23 20
fax 061/125 33 02

General Consulate
66 000 Koper, Belvedere 2
tel. 066/38 411, 38 412
fax 066/38 416

LIBERIA
64220 Bled, Koroška 11
tel. 064/77 009
fax 064/78 389

MACEDONIA
Ljubljana, Dunajska 104
tel. 061/168 44 54, 168 54 54
fax 061/168 51 81

NORWAY
Ljubljana, Dalmatinova 10
tel. 061/327 410
fax 061/327 330

POLAND
Ljubljana, Avčinova 4
tel. 061/132 02 09
fax 061/132 03 39

ROMANIA
Ljubljana, Nanoška 8
tel. in fax 061/268 702

RUSSIAN FEDERATION
Ljubljana, Rožna dolina, Cesta II/7
tel. 061/123 12 36, 123 26 63
fax 061/125 41 41

SWEDEN
Ljubljana, Dunajska 107
tel. 061/168 33 91
fax 061/168 11 79

SWITZERLAND
61103 Ljubljana, Šmartinska 130
p. p. 83
tel. 061/140 52 31
fax 061/140 11 54

THAILAND
Ljubljana, Grafenauerjeva 39
tel. in fax 061/344 090

THE NETHERLANDS
Ljubljana, Dunajska 22
tel. 061/325 796, 328 978
fax 061/326 158, 324 749

TURKEY
Ljubljana-Bežigrad, Livarska 4
tel. 061/132 20 12, 132 41 15
fax 061/132 31 58

UNITED STATES OF AMERICA
Ljubljana, Pražakova 4
tel. 061/301 427, 301 472
fax 061/301 401

VATICAN
Nunciature of the Holy See
Ljubljana, Tabor 3
tel. 061/131 41 33
fax 061/131 51 30

Representative Offices of the Republic of Slovenia Abroad

ARGENTINA
Embassy of the RS
Olazabal 2060
1428 BUENOS AIRES
tel. in fax 0054 1 1 781 7740

AUSTRALIA
Embassy of the RS
P.O.Box 284
60 Marcus Clarke Street
CANBERRA ACT 2601
tel. 0061 6 243 4830
fax 0061 6 243 4827

AUSTRIA
Botschaft der RS
Nibelungengasse 13
A-1010 WIEN
tel. 0043 1 586 1304, 0043 1 586 1307
fax 0043 1 586 1265

Generalkonsulat der RS
Bahnhofstr. 22
9020 KLAGENFURT
tel. 0043 463 54 150, 463 54 143
fax 0043 463 50 4071

BELGIUM
Ambassade de la RS
Avenue Marnix 30
1000 BRUXELLES
tel. 0032 2 646 90 99,
0032 2 646 90 84
fax 0032 2 646 36 67

CANADA
Embassy of the RS
150 Metcalfe Street, Suite 2101
OTTAWA, Ontario K2P 1P1
tel. 001 613 565 5781,
001 613 565 5782
fax 001 613 565 5783

CHINA
Embassy of the RS
23, Jian Guo Men Wai Da Jie
3-53, Jian Guo Men Wai Dipl.
Residence
100600 BEIJING
tel. 0086 1 532 6356, 0086 1 532 6357
fax 0086 1 532 6358

CROATIA
Ambasada RS
Savska cesta 41/IX
41000 ZAGREB
tel. 00385 41 517 401
fax 00385 41 517 837

CZECH REPUBLIC
Embassy of the RS
Pod hradbami 15
160 00 PRAGA 6
tel. 0042 2 341 431, 0042 2 341 325
fax 0042 2 320 864

EGYPT
Embassy of the RS
P. O. BOX 124, Magless
EL SHAAB OFFICE
5 Midon EL SARAYA EL KOUBRA
Garden City, CAIRO
tel. 0020 23 55 57 98
fax 0020 23 55 87 81

FRANCE
Ambassade de la RS
21, Bouquet de Longchamp
75116 PARIS
tel. 0033 1 47 55 65 90
fax 0033 1 47 55 60 05

Consulat général de la RS
40, allée de la Robertsau
67000 STRASBOURG
tel. 0033 88 366 025
fax 0033 88 371 444

GERMANY
Botschaft der RS
Siegfriedstr. 28
53179 BONN
tel. 0049 228 85 80 33,
9949 228 85 80 31
fax 0049 228 85 80 57

Generalkonsulat der RS
Lindwurmstr. 10
80045 MÜNCHEN 15
P.F. 150829
tel. 0040 89 543 9819
fax 0040 89 543 9483

GREAT BRITAIN
Embassy of the RS
Suite One, Cavendish Court
11-15 Wigmore Street
LONDON W1H 9LA
tel. 0044 71 495 7775
fax 0044 71 495 7776

GREECE
Embassy of the RS
Paleo Psychico, Mavili 10
154 52 ATHINA
tel. 0030 1 68 75 683,
0030 1 68 75 684
fax 0030 1 68 75 680

HUNGARY
A szlovén köztarsaság nagykövetsége
Cseppkö utca 68
1062 BUDAPEST
tel. 0036 1 250 8196, 0036 1 250 8180
fax 0036 1 250 8240

IRAN
Embassy of the RS
Khaled Eslamboli Ave,
7th Street
No. 10, 15989, TEHERAN
tel. 0098 21 871 68 73
fax 0098 21 872 04 74

ISRAEL
Embassy of the RS
2 Kaufman Street,
Textile House/12 Floor
68 012 TEL AVIV
tel. 0097 23 516 35 30,
0097 23 516 35 34
fax 0097 23 516 34 26

ITALY
Ambasciata della RS
Via Leonardo Pisano 10
00197 ROMA
tel. 0039 6 8081 075, 0039 6 8081 272
fax 0039 6 8081 471

Consolato generale della RS
p.p. 48, 66281 Škofije
Via Carducci 29
34100 TRIESTE
tel. 0039 40 636 161, 0039 40 636 488
fax 0039 40 636 272

JAPAN
Embassy of the RS
5-15 Akasaka 7-Chome
Minato-Ku, Tokyo 107
tel. 0081 3 5570 6275
fax 0081 3 5570 6075

MACEDONIA
Ambasada na RS
Bulevar Partizanski odredi 3
91000 SKOPJE
tel. 00389 91 116 213,
00389 91 220 112
fax 00389 91 118 006

POLAND
Embassy of the RS
Jakuba Kubieckega 9/m.6
02-954 WARSZAWA
tel. 0048 22 203 785
fax 0048 22 203 203

RUSSIAN FEDERATION
Embassy of the RS
Gruzinsky pereulok, dom 3, kv 41
123056 MOSKVA
tel. 0070 95 254 3531
fax 0070 95 254 7223

SPAIN
Embassy of the RS
Salustiano Olózaga 5, IV
28 001 MADRID
tel. 0034 1 575 65, 0034 1 575 88
fax 0034 1 575 00 91

SWEDEN
Embassy of the RS
Klarabergsgatan 33/II
111 21 STOCKHOLM
tel. 0046 8 21 8921, 0046 8 21 7980
fax 0046 8 723 0175

SWITZERLAND
UNO – Mission permanente de la RS
147, Rue de Lausanne (7e étage)
1202 GENEVE
tel. 0041 22 738 66 60,
0041 22 738 66 66
fax 0041 22 738 66 65

Botschaft der RS
Schwanengasse 9/II, 3011 BERN
tel. 0041 31 312 44 18
fax 0041 31 312 44 14

UNITED NATIONS
Permanent Mission of RS to the UN
600 Third Avenue, 24th Floor
NEW YORK, N.Y. 10016
tel. 001 212 370 3007
fax 001 212 370 1824

UNITED STATES OF AMERICA
Embassy of the RS
1525 New Hampshire Avenue, N.W.
WASHINGTON, D.C. 20036
tel. 001 202 667 5363
fax 001 202 667 4563

Consulate General of the RS
600 Third Avenue, 24th Floor
NEW YORK, N.Y. 10016
tel. 001 212 370 3006
fax 001 212 370 3581

VATICAN
Embassy of the RS to the Holy See
Via della Conciliazione, 10
00193 ROMA
tel. 0039 6 683 3009, 0039 6 687 8850
fax 0039 6 683 07 942

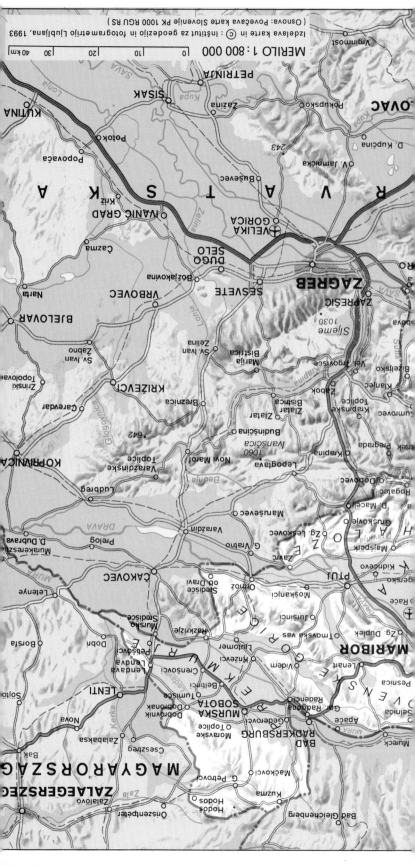